MW01134693

Enterprise Continuous Testing

Transforming Testing for Agile and DevOps

By Wolfgang Platz

With Cynthia Dunlop

Table of Contents

Foreword

By Clark Golestani

Previously President of Emerging Businesses and Global CIO for Merck, and presently the Managing Director of C Sensei Group.

With "digital" becoming part of every aspect of activity, brand, and reputation for a business, software testing has become vital. Yet, in this digital age, the amount of manual effort that goes into testing is incredible. I don't think any business process is as manual as software testing. The hands-on nature of software testing—even at software companies—is simply amazing. I have more automation in my coffee maker than most enterprises have in their testing processes. This is not only expensive; it also holds back innovation.

When you modernize testing for your digital initiatives, testing is elevated from being a line item on your P&L to something that's strategically critical going forward. By transforming testing, you can actually bridge the gaps in bimodal/two-speed IT—dramatically accelerating the "slower" speed and enabling the entire organization to move much faster.

Testing ensures that a digital asset will perform in the way you expect … or hope that it does. Yet testing has often been viewed as a necessary evil. It was just something you needed to do in order to get things released and paid for. It was never deemed strategic. This perspective came from the classic, waterfall approach to developing software, where testing was often outsourced. But the reality today is that that world is long gone.

Now, the move to DevOps and Agile methodologies has made testing an absolutely critical component of development activity. Continuous Testing becomes center stage to that product and needs to be integrated at every level, from the beginning through all of the continuous release cycles.

Along with a better product, you gain other benefits. You start to uncover development areas where you can create incredible levels of productivity gains, produce far better digital products, and save money—all at the same time.

The bottom line is that if you don't treat testing as a strategic initiative that's imperative to your digital success, your lunch is going to get eaten by your competitors. I don't think any leader can afford to take their eye off software testing.

Preface

Let's face it. Businesses don't want—or need—perfect software. They want to deliver innovations as soon as possible. A single delay might be the only opportunity a competitor needs to gain market share and become the new disruptor.

Testing is essential for accelerating the delivery of innovative applications without incurring unacceptable business risk. We need fast feedback on whether the latest innovations will work as expected or crash and burn in production. We also need to know if these changes somehow broke the core functionality that the customer base—and thus the business—depends upon.

However, even with the most extreme automation, we simply don't have time for the "test everything" approach. It's impossible to test every possible path through a modern business application every time that we want to release. Fortunately, we don't need to. If we rethink our testing approach, we can get a thorough assessment of a release candidate's business risk with much less testing than most companies are doing today.

Enterprise Continuous Testing: Transforming Testing for Agile and DevOps introduces a Continuous Testing strategy that helps enterprises accelerate and prioritize testing to meet the needs of fast-paced Agile and DevOps initiatives. Software testing has traditionally been the enemy of speed and innovation—a slow, costly process that delays releases while delivering questionable business value. This new strategy helps you test smarter, so testing provides rapid insight into what matters most to the business. It repositions testing from a bottleneck to a trusted advisor. Instead of the referee interrupting your progress for some trivial issue, testing becomes your coach, helping you push your limits and surge ahead of the competition.

Target Audience

This book is written for senior quality managers and business executives who need to achieve the optimal balance between speed and quality when delivering the software that drives the modern business. It provides a road-map for how to accelerate delivery with high confidence and low business risk.

Note that my focus is on functional testing. Developer-level Continuous Testing (featuring unit testing, the foundation of the famous inverted test pyramid, as well as practices such as static analysis and peer code review) is certainly important. However, these "Development Testing" best practices are already reasonably well-documented and understood. The place where organizations inevitably get stuck is functional testing—especially end-to-end functional testing.

Moreover, the struggles and strategies discussed throughout the book are targeted to Global 2000 companies. Most Continuous Testing success stories are heavily drawn from the so-called unicorns, but most businesses are not unicorns. Their reality includes complex legacy architectures, stringent compliance requirements, and a long history of manual testing. How can these organizations reinvent their testing processes to support Agile and DevOps—without slowing innovation or disrupting business-critical operations? That's the primary question this book aims to answer.

In summary: If you want to realign your Global 2000 organization's quality process with the unrelenting drive towards accelerated delivery speed and "Continuous Everything," then you're in the right place.

Acknowledgments

Many people were involved in developing this book, as well as the practice and methodology that underlies it. Special thanks are due to Wayne Ariola, Jordan Grantham, Teisha Grassberger, and Elmar Pauwels for their assistance in reviewing and preparing this book. It's also important to recognize the contributions of Sandeep Johri, Clark Golestani, Elmar Juergens, Tim Koopmans, Alexander Mohr, Sreeja Nair, Mike Nemeth, Viktoria Praschl, Daniela Schauer, Georg Thurner, Chris Trueman, Mario Van Oyen, and Robert Wagner.

CHAPTER 1

Enterprise Continuous Testing

Today, "Digital Transformation" is driving enterprises to innovate at lightning speed. We need to dedicate resources to creating new sources of customer value while continuously increasing operational agility. Otherwise, we risk waking up one day to find out that even though we did nothing "wrong," we somehow lost.

The speed of Digital Transformation is already staggering, and it's only going to increase. To put this into some very concrete terms, consider that:

- There are 7.7 billion people in the world
- 4.5 billion have regular access to a toilet
- 5.5 billion own a mobile phone

All of a sudden, a huge number of people jumped from a very provincial lifestyle straight into digital times—creating a tremendous demand for more, and more innovative, software.

Anyone responsible for producing software knows that the traditional ways of developing and delivering software aren't adequate for meeting this new demand. Not long ago, most companies were releasing software annually or bi-annually. Now, iterations commonly last 2 weeks or less. While delivery cycle time is decreasing, the technical complexity required to deliver a positive user experience and maintain a competitive edge is increasing.

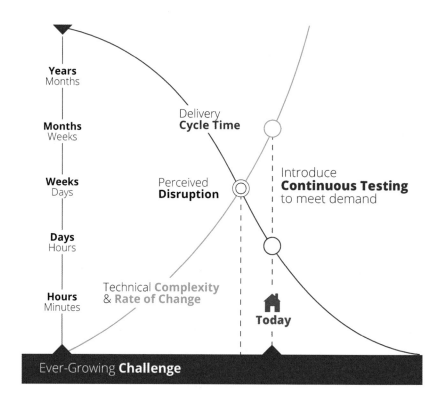

In terms of software testing, this brings us to an inflection point. In most organizations, testers were already racing to keep pace when delivery cycles were longer and application complexity was lower. Every quarter or so, the development team would pass a release candidate over the wall to QA, who would then scramble to validate it as thoroughly as possible in the allotted time—largely with manual testing.

Now, Digital Transformation initiatives such as Agile and DevOps are pushing traditional testing methods to their breaking point. Organizations are releasing much more frequently—from monthly on the low-end, to multiple times per hour on the high-end. Testers are expected to test each user story as soon as it's implemented (even when that functionality interacts with other functionality which is evolving in parallel). Additionally, testing is also expected to alert the team when the steady stream of changes unintentionally impacts the legacy functionality that was implemented, tested, and validated in previous weeks, months, or years. And as organizations increasingly edge towards Continuous Delivery with automated delivery pipelines, intermediary quality gates and the ultimate go/no-go decisions will all hinge upon test results.

Is your testing process up to the task?

Test automation is required, but it's not sufficient. When organizations adopt modern architectures and delivery methods, even teams with palpable test automation wins face roadblocks:

- They can't create and execute realistic tests fast enough or frequently enough

- They're overwhelmed by a seemingly never-ending stream of false positives and incomplete tests—not to mention all the test maintenance required to address them

- They can't confidently tell business leaders whether a release candidate is fit to be released

Testing must undergo its own digital transformation to meet the needs of modern Digital Transformation initiatives. This is where "Continuous Testing" comes into play.

What is Continuous Testing?

Continuous Testing is the process of executing automated tests as part of the software delivery pipeline in order to obtain feedback on the business risks associated with a software release as rapidly as possible. It evolves and extends test automation to address the increased complexity and pace of modern application development and delivery.

Continuous Testing really boils down to providing the right feedback to the right stakeholder at the right time. For decades, testing was traditionally deferred until the end of the cycle. At that point, testers would provide all sorts of important feedback...but nobody really wanted to hear it then. It was too late, and there was little the team could feasibly do, except delay the release. With Continuous Testing, the focus is on providing actionable feedback to people who really care about it—at the point when they are truly prepared to act on it.

DevOps is all about releasing differentiating software as efficiently as possible. Continuous Testing helps us achieve that by...

- Helping development teams identify and fix issues as efficiently as possible (accelerating innovation)

- Helping business leaders determine when it's reasonably safe to release (accelerating delivery)

This is achieved by mastering—and going beyond—test automation. It requires aligning testing with business risks, ensuring that testing effectively assesses the end user experience, and providing the instant quality feedback required at different stages of the delivery pipeline.

We Have a Problem (Two, Actually)

Unfortunately, we're not quite there yet. In most organizations, testing delays application delivery while providing limited insight into whether the applications under test are meeting stakeholder expectations. It's not fast enough to help teams find and fix defects when it's optimal to do so. And it's reporting on low-level test failures (e.g., 78% of our tests passed) rather than providing the business-focused perspective needed to make fast release decisions (e.g., Only 38% of our business risk was tested…and 25% of that didn't work properly).

Let's take a quick look at each of these problems in turn.

The Speed Problem

DevOps is all about removing the barriers to delivering innovative software faster. Yet, as other aspects of the delivery process are streamlined and accelerated, testing consistently emerges as the greatest limiting factor.

A recent GitLab survey that targeted developers and engineers found that testing is responsible for more delays than any other part of the development process.

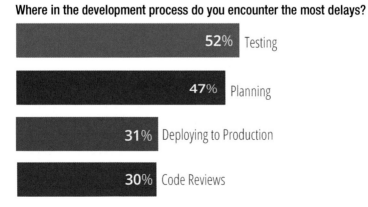

Where in the development process do you encounter the most delays?

52% Testing

47% Planning

31% Deploying to Production

30% Code Reviews

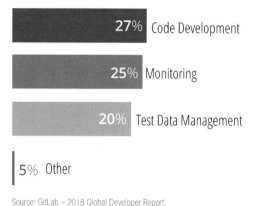

27% Code Development

25% Monitoring

20% Test Data Management

5% Other

Source: GitLab – 2018 Global Developer Report

The same conclusion was reached by a DevOps Review survey that polled a broader set of IT leaders across organizations practicing DevOps. Again, testing was cited as the #1 source of hold-ups in the software delivery process. In fact, testing "won" by a rather wide margin here. 63% reported that testing was a major source of delays; the second-highest source of delays (planning) was cited by only 32% of the respondents.

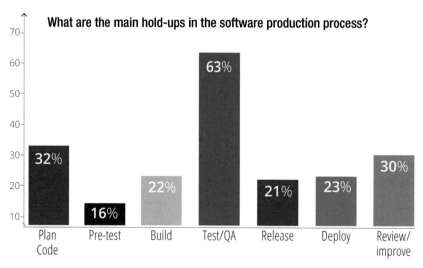

What are the main hold-ups in the software production process?

Source: Computing Research – DevOps Review

Why is testing such a formidable bottleneck? That could be the topic of another book. For now, let's summarize some key points:

- The vast majority of testing (over 80%) is still performed manually —even more at large enterprise organizations[1]

- Approximately 67% of the test cases being built, maintained, and executed are redundant and add no value to the testing effort[2]

- At the organizations that have significant test automation, testers spend 17% of their time dealing with false positives and another 14% on additional test maintenance tasks[3]

- Over half of testers spend 5-15 hours per week dealing with test data (average wait time for test data = 2 weeks)[4]

- 84% of testers are routinely delayed by limited test environment access (average wait time for test environments = 32 days)[5]

- The average regression test suite takes 16.5 days to execute, but the average Agile sprint is 2 weeks, from start to finish—including planning, implementation, and testing[6]

- The average application under test now interacts with 52 dependent systems—which means that a single end-to-end transaction could cross everything from microservices and APIs, to a variety of mobile

[1] Capgemini, Sogeti, HPE, World Quality Report 2018-19, 2019 (https://www.capgemini.com/service/world-quality-report-2018-19/).
[2] Tricentis research conducted from 2015-2018 at Global 2000 companies—primarily across finance, insurance, telecom, retail, and energy sectors.
[3] Tricentis research conducted from 2015-2018 at Global 2000 companies—primarily across finance, insurance, telecom, retail, and energy sectors.
[4] SDLC Partners Study, 2017 (https://sdlcpartners.com/point-of-view/test-data-management-chances-are-your-test-data-is-costing-you-more-time-and-money-than-you-know/).
[5] Delphix, State of Test Data Management, 2017 (https://www.delphix.com/white-paper/2017-state-test-data-management).
[6] Tricentis research conducted from 2015-2018 at Global 2000 companies—primarily across finance, insurance, telecom, retail, and energy sectors.

and browser interfaces, to packaged apps (SAP, Salesforce, Oracle, ServiceNow…), to custom/legacy applications, to mainframes[7]

The software testing process wasn't working perfectly even before the advent of Agile and DevOps. Now we're asking teams to "just speed it up" at the same time that modern application architectures are making testing even more complex. Given that, it's hardly surprising that speed expectations aren't being met.

The Insight Problem

Only 9% of companies perform formal risk assessments on their requirements/user stories. Most attempt to cover their top risks intuitively, and this results in an average business risk coverage of 40%.[8] Would you feel comfortable driving a race car with blinders on? That's essentially what you're doing if you're rapidly delivering software with insight into less than half of your total business risk.

Moreover, most organizations can't immediately differentiate between a test failure for a trivial issue and a business-critical failure that must be addressed immediately. Without an automated means of gaining this insight, you can't trust automated quality gates to stop high-risk candidates from progressing through the delivery pipeline. Human review will be required at each decision point—slowing the process and undermining the ultimate goal of release automation.

---

[7] Bas Dijkstra, Service Virtualization, O'Reilly, 2017 (https://www.oreilly.com/webops-perf/free/service-virtualization.csp).
[8] Tricentis research conducted from 2015-2018 at Global 2000 companies—primarily across finance, insurance, telecom, retail, and energy sectors.

Closing the Gap

How do you evolve from the slow, burdensome testing that delivers questionable results to the lean, streamlined testing that provides DevTest team members, as well as IT leaders, the fast feedback they need to accelerate innovation and delivery? That's what I aim to outline in the following chapters.

Read on to learn how to:

- Prioritize requirements by risk—so you can test the top ones first
- Design tests that cover your risks as efficiently as possible
- Automate tests rapidly, with minimal maintenance
- See the risk impact of your test failures
- Identify critical "blind spots" that are not yet tested
- Prepare your automation for constant, consistent execution within CI
- Balance test automation with creative exploration

CHAPTER 2

A New Currency for Testing: Risk

If you've ever looked at test results, you've probably seen something like this:

What does this really tell you?

You know that…

- There's a total of 53,274 tests cases
- Almost 80% of those tests (42,278) passed
- Over 19% of them failed
- About 1% did not execute

But…would you be willing to make (or recommend) a release decision based on these results? Maybe the test failures are related to some trivial functionality. Maybe they stem from the most critical functionality: the "engine" of your system. Or, maybe your most critical functionality was not even tested at all. Trying to track down this information would require tons of manual investigative work that yields delayed, often-inaccurate answers.

In the era of Agile and DevOps, release decisions need to be made rapidly—even automatically and instantaneously. Test results that focus on the number of test cases leave you with a huge blind spot that becomes absolutely critical—and incredibly dangerous—when you're moving at the speed of Agile and DevOps.

A New Currency for Testing

Test coverage wouldn't be such a bad metric if all application functions and all tests were equally important. However, they're not. Focusing on the number of tests without considering the importance of the functionality they're testing is like focusing on the number of stocks you own without any insight into their valuations.

Based on the test results shown above, you can't tell if the release will ignite a "software fail" scenario that gets your organization into the headlines for all the wrong reasons. If you want fast, accurate assessments of the risks associated with promoting the latest release candidate to production, you need a new currency in testing: risk coverage needs to replace test coverage.

Test coverage tells you what percentage of the total application functions are covered by test cases. Each application has a certain number of functions; let's call that n functions:

$$F_1 - F_n$$

However, you probably won't have time to test all n functions. You can test only m of the available n functions:

$$F_1 - F_m \ m \leq n$$

You would calculate your test coverage as follows:

$$TC = \frac{m}{n}\,[\%]$$

For instance, if you have 200 functions but tested only 120 of those functions, this gives you 60% test coverage:

$$TC = \frac{120}{200}\,[60\%]$$

Risk coverage tells you what percentage of your business risk is covered by test cases. Risk coverage accounts for the fact that some tests are substantially more important than others, and thus have a higher *risk weight* than the others (we'll explore exactly how risk weights are determined in the next chapter).

With risk coverage, the focus shifts from the *number* of requirements tested to the *risk weight* of the requirements tested. You can usually achieve much higher risk coverage by testing 10 critical requirements than you can by testing 100 more trivial ones.

The sum of all risk weights always totals 100%:

$$\sum_{i=1}^{n} w_i = 100\%$$

If you add up the risk weights for the *m* requirements that have been tested, this gives you the risk coverage *RC*:

$$RC_{\;m\leq n} = \sum_{i=1}^{m} w_i$$

For a simple example, assume that the risk weights of your core requirements are as follows (we'll take a deep dive into risk weighting in the next chapter):

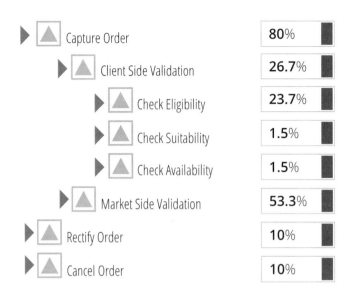

If you fully cover the Capture Order requirement, you'll achieve 80% risk coverage. If you cover the Rectify Order and Cancel Order requirements, you'll achieve only 20% risk coverage. In other words, you get 4X the amount of risk coverage with half as much work. This is a prime example of "test smarter, not harder."

By measuring risk coverage, you gain insight into:

1. How rigorously your top business risks were tested
2. Whether your top risks are meeting expectations (based on the correlated testing outcomes)
3. The severity of your "blind spot": the percentage of your business risk that is not tested at all

For example, consider the following results:

Risk Coverage [%]

Core Bank	66%	9%	15%	10%

We don't worry about the number of test cases here because we have much more powerful insight: we can tell that only 66% of our Core Bank business risk is tested and appears to be working as expected. Additionally, we know that the functionality for 9% of our business risk seems to be broken, the functionality for 15% of our business risk has tests that aren't running, and the functionality for 10% of our business risk doesn't have any tests at all. This means that at least 9%—and potentially 34%—of the functionality for our business risk is not working in this release.

Would you rather know this…or that 53,274 tests were executed and almost 80% passed?

Now, let's return to our earlier question: are you confident promoting this release to production?

All Tests Are Not Created Equal

The reason why traditional test results are such a poor predictor of release readiness boils down to the 80/20 rule (i.e., the Pareto principle). Most commonly, this refers to the idea that *20% of the effort creates 80% of the value.*

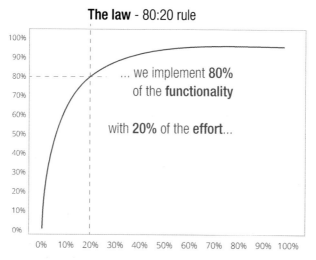

The software development equivalent is that 20% of your transactions represent 80% of your business value…and that tests for 20% of your requirements can cover 80% of your business risk.

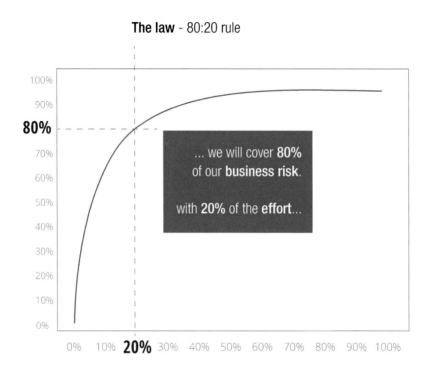

Most teams already recognize that some functionality is more important to the business, and they aim to test it more thoroughly than functionality they perceive to be more trivial. Taking the alternative path—trying to test all functionality equally, regardless of its perceived risk—soon becomes a Sisyphean effort. With this route, you quickly approach the "critical limit": the point where the time required to execute the tests exceeds the time available for test execution.

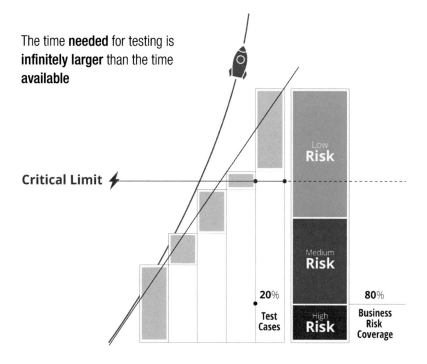

The time **needed** for testing is **infinitely larger** than the time available

Critical Limit

Low **Risk**

Medium **Risk**

High **Risk**

20% Test Cases

80% Business Risk Coverage

However, when teams try to intuitively cover the highest risks more thoroughly, they tend to achieve only 40% risk coverage, and end up accumulating a test suite that has a high degree of redundancy (a.k.a. "bloat"). On average, 67% of tests don't contribute to risk coverage—but they make the test suite slow to execute and difficult to maintain.

As the next chapter will explain, once you achieve an accurate assessment of where your risks lie, you can cover those risks extremely efficiently. This is a huge untapped opportunity to make your testing more impactful. If you understand how risk is distributed across your application and you know which 20% of your transactions are correlated to that 80% of your business value, it's entirely feasible to cover your top business risks without an exorbitant testing investment. This translates to a test suite that's faster to create and execute, as well as less work to maintain. Add in the appropriate automation and correlation, and you'll reach the "holy grail": fast feedback on whether a release has an acceptable level of business risk.

CHAPTER 3

Use Risk Prioritization to Focus Testing

Many organizations think that this risk-based approach to testing sounds great in theory, but doubt that they can really achieve it—especially given the limited downtime available with today's unrelenting, fast-paced development iterations. Understanding and targeting the top business risks is actually a relatively simple and painless process. In fact, we've found that the less time you spend on it, the better the results.

In this chapter, I'll explain how you can systematically identify your top risks in a matter of hours. This is a foundational step for 1) determining where to focus your testing efforts and 2) monitoring how well your business risks are tested—and whether they are actually working as expected.

Defining Risk

Before diving into how to assess your top risks and cover them as efficiently as possible, let's first take a step back and consider what risk really means.

At its most basic level, **risk** quantifies the potential of losing something of value—and "business risk" quantifies the potential of negatively impacting

17

the business. This "negative impact" could manifest itself in terms of lost revenue, brand erosion, falling stock prices, diminished internal productivity, and so on.

Business risk is determined by the following formula:

Risk = Frequency × Damage

Frequency is a measure of how often the associated item (requirement, user story, etc.) is used. Is it part of almost every core business transaction or is it used only in fairly specialized cases?

Damage is a measure of the potential damage that could result from the failure of the associated item. Would it prevent a core transaction from proceeding? Would there be significant financial impacts? Would it simply cause an inconvenience with an intuitive workaround? Or, would it lead to regulatory non-compliance?

Ultimately, the more frequently something is used and the more damage that its failure could cause, the higher the risk. For example, a rarely-used payment type option might have a higher risk than a commonly-used customization option (e.g., change the application's UI colors to "dark mode").

Assessing Your Application's Risks

At Tricentis, we've spent 8 years developing, testing, and fine-tuning a process for helping organizations rapidly assess the business risk of their applications' various components (requirements, epics, user stories, etc.). Here is the rapid assessment process we've found to deliver the best results.

Step 1: Stakeholder Commitment

Get several key stakeholders to commit to a 1.5 day meeting with someone to guide them through the risk assessment process.

> **Note:** Rather than recruit the business analysts for this task, it's usually easier—and more effective—to have business testers complete the requirements review (Step 2) and risk ranking (Step 3). The business testers then send the initial ranking to the business analysts for review (Step 4).

Step 2: Requirements Review

Briefly review the requirements, epics, user stories, etc. for the application under test (in this book, I'll use the terms "requirements" and "subrequirements" as catch-alls for all the possible options). If you have a fairly complex system, you might want to initially focus on the epic level instead of the user story level to keep the granularity manageable.

You don't have to address every requirement when you're just starting off. Focus on covering the main business objects and elementary use cases. For example, business objects might be customer, contract, car, etc. Elementary use cases might be create, administer (e.g., increase, decrease), and delete.

Details			
Name	Frequency class	Damage class	Weight
Demo Web Shop			
Customer Tasks	4	4	256
Register	3	4	128
Login	5	4	512
Modify Customer Data	3	2	32
Check Orders	2	3	32
Handle Products	3	3	64
Product Configuration	3	3	64
Modify Products View	4	2	64
Compare Products	1	1	4
Search for Products	4	2	64

Step 3: Risk Ranking

First, rank the requirements based on their actual or anticipated usage frequency. Start by selecting the most frequently used requirement and rank it a 5. Next, rank the least frequently used requirement a 1. Then, rate the others by comparing them to the most and least frequently used ones. The frequency should double at each stage; for example, 2 is twice as frequent as 1, 3 is twice as frequent as 2, …

Next, repeat the same process for damage: the amount of damage that could ensue if this requirement failed. Again, start by selecting the requirements that could cause the greatest and least damage, then use those two extremes to rate the others.

The goal is to end up with an assessment like this:

	Frequency	Damage
Req critical	5	5
Req B	5	4
Req C	4	4
Req D	2	5
.	.	.
.	.	.
.	.	.
Req trivial	1	1

Note that the ranking should be completed incrementally, hierarchy level by hierarchy level. You start with the top-level requirements, then move to the next level below that, and so on.

Step 4: Ranking Review

Once the process is completed, give other interested parties the opportunity to review the risk ranking results—with the warning that if you don't receive any feedback within a week, you'll start using the current ratings and be open to revisiting the ratings later.

Step 5: Calculating Risk Contributions

Once the risks for each requirement are settled, you'll want to use them to determine the risk contribution of each layer of your requirement structure—as well as the tests associated with each layer of that structure.

First, you calculate the risk weight. I mentioned earlier that you get the risk level by multiplying the frequency and damage values. For example:

	Frequency	Damage	Risk
Very low	1	1	1
.	.	.	.
.	.	.	.
.	.	.	.
Very high	5	5	25

If you're rating frequency and damage on a scale of 1 to 5, this gives you a minimum risk of 1 (very low frequency and very low damage) and a maximum risk of 25 (very high frequency and very high damage). This results in a risk spread of 1:25.

However, the risk spread of business value across most enterprise systems is actually much greater than that. Research has shown that in large enterprises, the least critical functionality is 0.4 the importance of the most critical functionality. This is a factor of 250—so we need to amplify the spread between very high risk and very low risk accordingly.

The following formula will get you extremely close to that (1:256), so that's the approach I recommend:

$$Absolute\ Weight = 2^{Frequency} \times 2^{Damage}$$

With this approach, the frequency and damage are expressed as follows:

	Frequency	Damage	Risk
Very low	2^1	2^1	
.	.	.	.
.	.	.	.
.	.	.	.
Very high	2^5	2^5	

This changes the risk calculations to:

	Frequency	Damage	Risk	
Very low	2	2	4	1
.			.	
.	.	.	.	$\triangleq$
.			.	
Very high	32	32	1024	256

The result is a risk spread of 4:1024—which is the equivalent of 1:256.

Once you understand the concept behind these rankings, you can use automation (e.g., via a Continuous Testing platform like the Tricentis platform) to streamline the process—especially if you are working with many requirements. For example, assume you were performing a risk assessment for a retail application. If your requirements were specified in a requirements management system like Atlassian Jira, you would sync them into your Continuous Testing platform. Next, you would specify the frequency and damage for each item. The risk (i.e., absolute weight) would then be calculated automatically.

Name	Frequency class	Damage class	Weight
Details			
▲ Demo Web Shop			
▲ Customer Tasks	4	4	256
▲ Register	3	4	128
▲ Login	5	4	512
▲ Modify Customer Data	3	2	32
▲ Check Orders	2	3	32
▲ Handle Products	3	3	64
▲ Product Configuration	3	3	64
▲ Modify Products View	4	2	64
▲ Compare Products	1	1	4
▲ Search for Products	4	2	64
▲ Shopping Cart	5	5	1024
▲ Add Products	3	5	256
▲ Gift Cards	3	4	128
▲ Discounts	3	4	128
▲ Manage Shopping Cart	3	4	128
▲ Order Process	5	5	1024
▲ Execute Checkout	3	5	256
▲ Billing and Shipping Address	2	5	128
▲ Calculate Shipping Costs	5	5	1024
▲ Payment Methods	5	5	1024
▲ Re-Order	2	4	64

From the **absolute weights**, you can determine the **relative weight**: the weighting of each requirement relative to all other requirements on the same hierarchical level. Here, the *Calculate Shipping Costs* subrequirement accounts for 41% of its parent *Order Process* requirement. The relative weights <u>at any given hierarchical</u> level will always add up to 100%.

Name	Frequency class	Damage class	Weight	Relative Weight (%)
Details				
▲ Demo Web Shop				
▲ Customer Tasks	4	4	256	10,81
▲ Handle Products	3	3	64	2,7
▲ Shopping Cart	5	5	1024	43,24
▲ Order Process	5	5	1024	43,24
▲ Execute Checkout	3	5	256	10,26
▲ Billing and Shipping Address	2	5	128	5,13
▲ Calculate Shipping Costs	5	5	1024	41,03
▲ Payment Methods	5	5	1024	41,03
▲ Re-Order	2	4	64	2,56

You can also determine the **Business risk contribution percentage**, which indicates how much each element in the requirement hierarchy contributes to the overall application risk. The Business risk contribution percentage across *all* available hierarchical levels will add up to 100%.

Details

Name	Frequency class	Damage class	Weight	Relative Weight (%)	Contribution (%)
Demo Web Shop					
Customer Tasks	4	4	256	10,81	10,81
Register	3	4	128	18,18	1,97
Login	5	4	512	72,73	7,86
Modify Customer Data	3	2	32	4,55	0,49
Check Orders	2	3	32	4,55	0,49
Handle Products	3	3	64	2,7	2,7
Product Configuration	3	3	64	32,65	0,88
Modify Products View	4	2	64	32,65	0,88
Compare Products	1	1	4	2,04	0,06
Search for Products	4	2	64	32,65	0,88
Shopping Cart	5	5	1024	43,24	43,24
Add Products	3	5	256	40	17,3
Gift Cards	3	4	128	20	8,65
Discounts	3	4	128	20	8,65
Manage Shopping Cart	3	4	128	20	8,65
Order Process	5	5	1024	43,24	43,24
Execute Checkout	3	5	256	10,26	4,44
Billing and Shipping Address	2	5	128	5,13	2,22
Calculate Shipping Costs	5	5	1024	41,03	17,74
Payment Methods	5	5	1024	41,03	17,74
Re-Order	2	4	64	2,56	1,11

For example, the *Calculate Shipping Costs* subrequirement that accounts for 41% of its parent *Order Process* requirement also accounts for 18% of the total application risk.

Assessment Complete...Now What?

When the risk assessment is completed, you should have a crystal-clear understanding of where your greatest risks lie. Your next challenge: covering your top risks as efficiently as possible. There are two parts to this:

1. Determining **where** to add tests to establish acceptable coverage of your top business risks

2. Determining **how** to add tests so that they cover the targeted business risks as efficiently as possible

The first part involves determining what's most critical to test. If you're starting from scratch, plan to begin by testing your highest risk, then work back from there as your resources permit. If you have existing tests, correlate them to your risk-weighted requirements and run them. This will give you a baseline of your existing risk coverage—and insight into the gaps you should work to fill.

For example, assume you're expected to start testing the following application, and you have time to test only half of your requirements before the upcoming release.

Details

Name	Frequency class	Damage class	Weight	Relative Weight (%)	Contribution (%)
Demo Web Shop					
Customer Tasks	4	4	256	10,81	10,81
Register	3	4	128	18,18	1,97
Login	5	4	512	72,73	7,86
Modify Customer Data	3	2	32	4,55	0,49
Check Orders	2	3	32	4,55	0,49
Handle Products	3	3	64	2,7	2,7
Product Configuration	3	3	64	32,65	0,88
Modify Products View	4	2	64	32,65	0,88
Compare Products	1	1	4	2,04	0,06
Search for Products	4	2	64	32,65	0,88
Shopping Cart	5	5	1024	43,24	43,24
Add Products	3	5	256	40	17,3
Gift Cards	3	4	128	20	8,65
Discounts	3	4	128	20	8,65
Manage Shopping Cart	3	4	128	20	8,65
Order Process	5	5	1024	43,24	43,24
Execute Checkout	3	5	256	10,26	4,44
Billing and Shipping Address	2	5	128	5,13	2,22
Calculate Shipping Costs	5	5	1024	41,03	17,74
Payment Methods	5	5	1024	41,03	17,74
Re-Order	2	4	64	2,56	1,11

Which do you want to tackle first? If you choose *Order Process* and *Shopping Cart*, you'll cover over 80% of the application's risk. But if you choose *Customer Tasks* and *Handle Products*, you'll cover around 10% of the application's risk—with the same level of testing effort. When you have this insight into risk contribution, it's simple to make smart tradeoffs on how to best utilize the limited testing time available.

Once you start adding tests (the next chapter will cover this in detail), linking them to requirements will help you identify the risk contribution of each test. Moreover, this correlation between tests, requirements, and risk is essential for obtaining risk-based reporting. With everything linked and correlated, you'll gain insight into:

- Prominent gaps in your risk coverage
- The business impact of your test failures
- The readiness of particular requirements
- The application's overall release readiness

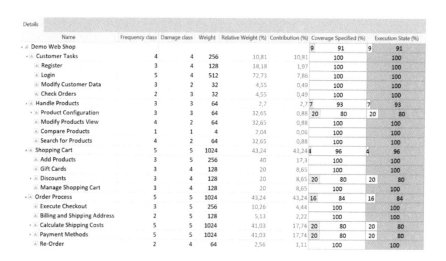

Details

Name	Frequency class	Damage class	Weight	Relative Weight (%)	Contribution (%)		Coverage Specified (%)		Execution State (%)
Demo Web Shop						9	91	9	91
Customer Tasks	4	4	256	10,81	10,81		100		100
Register	3	4	128	18,18	1,97		100		100
Login	5	4	512	72,73	7,86		100		100
Modify Customer Data	3	2	32	4,55	0,49		100		100
Check Orders	2	3	32	4,55	0,49		100		100
Handle Products	3	3	64	2,7	2,7	7	93	7	93
Product Configuration	3	3	64	32,65	0,88	20	80	20	80
Modify Products View	4	2	64	32,65	0,88		100		100
Compare Products	1	1	4	2,04	0,06		100		100
Search for Products	4	2	64	32,65	0,88		100		100
Shopping Cart	5	5	1024	43,24	43,24	4	96	4	96
Add Products	3	5	256	40	17,3		100		100
Gift Cards	3	4	128	20	8,65		100		100
Discounts	3	4	128	20	8,65	20	80	20	80
Manage Shopping Cart	3	4	128	20	8,65		100		100
Order Process	5	5	1024	43,24	43,24	16	84	16	84
Execute Checkout	3	5	256	10,26	4,44		100		100
Billing and Shipping Address	2	5	128	5,13	2,22		100		100
Calculate Shipping Costs	5	5	1024	41,03	17,74	20	80	20	80
Payment Methods	5	5	1024	41,03	17,74	20	80	20	80
Re-Order	2	4	64	2,56	1,11		100		100

Once you know where to add tests, you'll want to design those tests in a way that achieves high risk coverage as efficiently as possible. This means that each test should have a distinct purpose and a clear contribution to risk coverage—and that any tests which do not add value should be removed to accelerate execution speed and streamline test maintenance. The next chapter outlines a methodology for accomplishing that.

Alternative Assessment Approaches

Seem too simple? We (Tricentis) thought so, too. That's why we applied and compared three different approaches across telecom and insurance companies:

- The rapid assessment method outlined here
- A deep dive where a larger group of business analysts reviewed and challenged the results of the rapid assessment
- A review of real data on frequency and damages

Here's how the 3 different approaches compared:

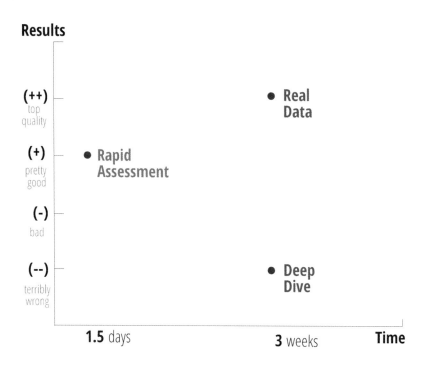

Why did the deep dive approach deliver such poor results? Political correctness. Telling someone that "their" functionality is not as important as other functionality is like telling them that their baby is ugly. With all the business analysts sitting together and trying to avoid offending one another, you end up with essentially the same weights for all the requirements. This negates the value of the entire exercise.

Not surprisingly, assessments based on actual frequency and damage data provided the top-quality results. However, this approach required 10X as much time, given all the data collection and correlation that was required. It was more accurate, but not 10X better. In most cases, you won't even have the option of accessing real damage and frequency data. But even if you do have access to it, think about whether the time required to collect and correlate it all is really worth it.

Updating the Risk Assessment in Each Iteration

Of course, when you're working in an Agile process, you're going to have new requirements every couple of weeks. However, you don't want to add those new requirements into the core risk structure—not at first, at least.

When you start a new sprint (ideally, during the planning meeting), you create a list of user stories for that sprint and compare them against *one another*—not against all the other requirements that are already in your risk structure. Why? Because new functionality is more likely to fail than functionality that you have already checked and verified. All new functionality introduced in a given sprint will be riskier than your existing functionality (progression testing vs. regression testing). The weighting will help you determine how to allocate your limited in-sprint testing time among the various new user stories. All the new user stories are likely to have issues—but you want to focus your resources on testing the ones with the greatest risk potential.

For example, the in-sprint user story risk assessment might look like this:

Details			
Name	Frequency class	Damage class	Weight
Sprint #1			
US1: As a user, I want to order different products, ship them using different methods and pay the correct shipping fee	5	5	1024
US2: As a user, I want to order use different payment methods and pay the correct payment fee	5	4	512
US3: As a user, I want to use discount codes and have them applied correctly	2	4	64
US4: As a user, I want to adapt products myself and have the changes be reflected accordingly	2	3	32

Then, after all those user stories are verified and deemed "done done," you review the risk assessment again. This time, you re-rank the frequency and damage in relation to the larger risk structure. Now that these user stories have "graduated" from progression testing to regression testing, they should be ranked accordingly. This re-ranking will help you immediately understand the severity of a regression test failure.

CHAPTER 4

Design Tests for Highly-Efficient Risk Coverage

As the last chapter outlined, a risk-weighted assessment of your requirements and subrequirements helps you decide where to focus your testing efforts. Based on an assessment like the following, you might decide to start off by testing the subrequirements that have the greatest contribution to the overall risk coverage, then address the other subrequirements as time permits.

Name	Frequency class	Damage class	Weight	Relative Weight (%)	Contribution (%)
Demo Web Shop					
Customer Tasks	4	4	256	10,81	10,81
Register	3	4	128	18,18	1,97
Login	5	4	512	72,73	7,86
Modify Customer Data	3	2	32	4,55	0,49
Check Orders	2	3	32	4,55	0,49
Handle Products	3	3	64	2,7	2,7
Product Configuration	3	3	64	32,65	0,88
Modify Products View	4	2	64	32,65	0,88
Compare Products	1	1	4	2,04	0,06
Search for Products	4	2	64	32,65	0,88
Shopping Cart	5	5	1024	43,24	43,24
Add Products	3	5	256	40	17,3
Gift Cards	3	4	128	20	8,65
Discounts	3	4	128	20	8,65
Manage Shopping Cart	3	4	128	20	8,65
Order Process	5	5	1024	43,24	43,24
Execute Checkout	3	5	256	10,26	4,44
Billing and Shipping Address	2	5	128	5,13	2,22
Calculate Shipping Costs	5	5	1024	41,03	17,74
Payment Methods	5	5	1024	41,03	17,74
Re-Order	2	4	64	2,56	1,11

Once you know *what* to test, you need to determine *how* to test it. Now, you want to focus on achieving the greatest risk coverage for the targeted requirements as efficiently as possible.

We've already established that all requirements are not created equal (from a risk perspective). The same holds true for the tests created to validate those requirements. A single strategically-designed test can help you achieve as much, if not more, risk coverage than 10 other tests that were "intuitively" designed for the same requirement.

The goal of this chapter is to help you test your highest-risk requirements as efficiently as possible. This is accomplished with a "less is more" strategy. Strive for the fewest possible tests needed to 1) reach your risk coverage targets AND 2) ensure that when a test fails, you know exactly what application functionality to investigate.

If you already have a test suite for your highest-risk requirements, this exercise will help you identify gaps as well as eliminate redundant test cases that slow execution speed and add to your overall test maintenance burden.

Getting Started: Defining Equivalence Classes

Assume we have a simple auto insurance application that calculates the annual premium using the following business logic:
- Anyone younger than 18 years of age will not be insured
- Drivers between 18 and 23 pay a 10% surcharge
- Drivers 60 and older get a 5% discount
- Women get a 20% discount
- Drivers living in an urban city area pay a 15% surcharge

To start, you need to understand the dimensions of the problem—the attributes you need to focus on. The obvious attributes are:

- Age, which we will represent as a range from 0 to 100
- Gender, which has 2 options (male/female)
- Location, which has 2 options (city [urban] vs. country [rural])

If you wanted to test all possible combinations of Age (0-100), Gender (male or female) and Location (city or country), you would have 400 test cases:

$$100 \times 2 \times 2 = 400$$

However, there's no need to create 400 test cases. In fact, I'll show you how to achieve the same risk coverage and code coverage with just a handful of test cases.

The key to reducing the number of test cases required is understanding and applying *equivalence classes*. Each equivalence class represents a range of inputs that produce the same result in the application under test. Any value within an equivalence class is just as likely to expose a defect as any other value within that class—so there's no additional benefit of testing multiple different values within a given equivalence class. These tests are logically redundant, and it's typically not worth your time and effort to create, maintain, and execute them. In fact, their existence increases your test suite bloat—which is hardly going to help you achieve your goal of "lean" testing.

To really clarify this concept of equivalence classes, let's return to the insurance example and create equivalence classes for each range of attribute values that should produce the same result.

First, consider age.

- Based on the requirement *Anyone younger than 18 years of age will not be insured*, we can create one equivalence class for age < 18. It doesn't matter if the applicant is age 1, 6, 12, or 17. In all those cases, the application will be rejected.

- From the requirement *Drivers between 18 and 23 pay a 10% surcharge*, we can create another equivalence class for ages 18 to 23. Again, if you test the application for a 19-year-old driver, you don't also need to test it for drivers who are 18, 20, 21, 22, and 23.

- After reviewing the final age-related requirement *(Drivers 60 and older get a 5% discount)*, we would want to create two final equivalence classes for age: one for ages 24 to 59 and one for ages 60 and over. Any driver from age 24 to 59 will not receive any age-related surcharges or discounts. Moreover, any driver aged 60+ will receive the standard 5% senior discount.

In summary, this gives us the following equivalence classes for the age attribute:

- <18
- 18>23
- 24>59
- >59

With Tricentis' test design, these equivalence classes would be rendered as follows:

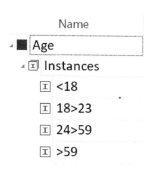

Why is it safe to assume that every value in an equivalence class produces the same result? Because all values in each equivalence class cover the same piece of code. Imagine the following (extremely simplified for demonstration purposes) piece of code:

```
switch case age

    case <18
      |____

    case 18>23
      |____

    case 24>59
      |____

    case else
      |____
```

To ensure that the age functionality is tested thoroughly, you need to cover all the case statements in the code. You can achieve that coverage with just four values—one that represents each of the four equivalence classes. For instance, you could use 16, 21, 45, and 70:

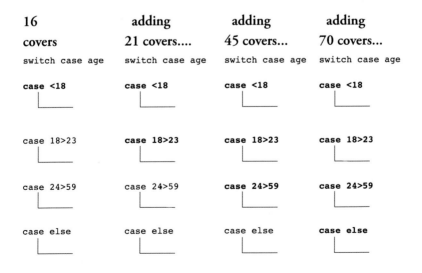

16 covers	**adding 21 covers....**	**adding 45 covers...**	**adding 70 covers...**
switch case age	switch case age	switch case age	switch case age
case <18	case <18	case <18	case <18
case 18>23	**case 18>23**	case 18>23	case 18>23
case 24>59	case 24>59	**case 24>59**	case 24>59
case else	case else	case else	**case else**

If you tested 16, 21, 45, and 70, there is no value added by testing additional age variations. Think of all the values you now do NOT need to test:

~~0~~ ~~1~~ ~~2~~ ~~3~~ ~~4~~ ~~5~~ ~~6~~ ~~7~~ ~~8~~ ~~9~~ ~~10~~ ~~11~~ ~~12~~ ~~13~~ ~~14~~ ~~15~~ **16** ~~17~~

~~18~~ ~~19~~ ~~20~~ **21** ~~22~~ ~~23~~

~~24~~ ~~25~~ ~~26~~ ~~27~~ ~~28~~ ~~29~~ ~~30~~ ~~31~~ ~~32~~ ~~33~~ ~~34~~ ~~35~~ ~~36~~ ~~37~~ ~~38~~ ~~39~~ ~~40~~ ~~41~~ ~~42~~ ~~43~~ ~~44~~ **45** ~~46~~ ~~47~~ ~~48~~ ~~49~~ ~~50~~ ~~51~~ ~~52~~ ~~53~~ ~~54~~ ~~55~~ ~~56~~ ~~57~~ ~~58~~ ~~59~~

~~60~~ ~~61~~ ~~62~~ ~~63~~ ~~64~~ ~~65~~ ~~66~~ ~~67~~ ~~68~~ ~~69~~ **70** ~~71~~ ~~72~~ ~~73~~ ~~74~~ ~~75~~ ~~76~~ ~~77~~ ~~78~~ ~~79~~ ~~80~~ ... ~~100~~

Testing any of those additional values in each equivalence class would require extra time to:
- Design the tests
- Automate the tests
- Run the tests
- Maintain the tests

All for no additional benefit.

The same concept applies for gender and location. These are both simpler than age because the options are binary (whereas age was a continuum). For gender, the (simplified) code is something like:

```
switch case gender

    case male

    case female
```

To cover this code, you need two attribute values: male and female. Each is an equivalence class.

Likewise, for location (urban/city vs. rural/country), the (simplified) code is:

```
switch case location
  case city
   |_____

  case country
   |_____
```

To cover this code, you need two attribute values: city and country. Again, each is an equivalence class.

In summary, the business logic in the above example yields the following equivalence classes:

- Age < 18
- Age 18-23
- Age 24-59
- Age > 59
- Male
- Female
- City (Urban)
- Country (Rural)

Since these are equivalence classes, we can select just one representative value from each class.

Combinatorics

Next, we want to cover all this logic—thoroughly and efficiently. Given that there are 4 age groups, 2 gender categories, and 2 location categories to test, the common assumption is that you need 16 tests (4 x 2 x 2) to cover everything. Fortunately, that's not the case. Actually, you can cover all that application logic with just 4 test cases if you take an "each choice," or *orthogonal*, approach to test design.

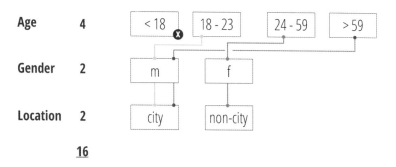

1. Age less than 18
2. Age between 18-23 + male + city (urban)
3. Age between 24 and 59 + female + country (rural)
4. Age greater than 59 + either male or female + either city (urban) or non-city (rural)

However, there's a problem. What if the second test passes and the third test fails? What functionality is failing: the 24-59 age group pricing, the discounted rates for females, or the discounted rates for non-city residents? Further testing would be required to hone in on exactly what failed. Although this solution is extremely efficient, it's not ideal.

Linear Expansion

Enter linear expansion. Linear expansion is *almost* as efficient as the above approach, and it also ensures that you can always determine what functionality was responsible for a given test failure.

With linear expansion, you begin with what's called the "happy path" or "straight through": the test that uses the most important attribute values and achieves the highest risk coverage. On average, the "straight through" covers 4X more of your risk than the other paths.

From the straight through, you vary just one attribute instance each time. Returning to our example, this approach gives us two additional tests:

Details	Relations						
Name		⬛ StraightThrough	⬛ Female	⬛ Country	⬛ 18>23	⬛ >59	⬛ <18
⬛ Linear Expansion		StraightThrough	Female	Country	18>23	>59	<18
▸ ⬛ Instances							
▸ ⬛ Age		⬛ 24>59	⬛ 24>59	⬛ 24>59	⬛ 18>23	⬛ >59	⬛ <18
▸ ⬛ Gender		⬛ Male	⬛ Female	⬛ Male	⬛ Male	⬛ Male	⬛ Male
▸ ⬛ Location		⬛ City	⬛ City	⬛ Country	⬛ City	⬛ City	⬛ City

1. Age 24-59 + male + city (straight through)
2. Age 24-59 + **female** + city
3. Age 24-59 + male + **country**
4. **Age 18-23** + male + city
5. **Age greater than 59** + male + city
6. **Age less than 18**

Attribute variations are bolded above.

Now, if a single test other than the "straight through" fails, we know exactly what application logic is failing: it's obviously the part of code related to the variation in the failed test.

For example, if all tests pass except for

Age greater than 59 + male + city

then we know that the code behind the *Drivers 60 and older get a 5% discount* requirement needs to be reviewed.

If all tests pass except for

Age 24-59 + **female** + city

then we know that the code behind the *Women get a 20% discount* requirement needs to be reviewed.

The only real constraint of linear expansion is that it assumes you can "mix and match" attribute values in any combination and still produce logical outcomes. That's often the case. However, some combinations just don't make sense—and, more importantly, certain application behavior cannot be triggered without a very specific combination of attributes.

For instance, assume that the insurance application needs to provide an additional 10% discount for drivers who are retired—but retirement age varies for men and women (as it does in Austria, where women retire at 60 and men retire at 65). In this case, a 64-year-old woman would receive the retirement discount, but a man of the same age would not.

Or, consider a couple of examples in the retail space: shipping costs vary according to product type (digital downloads incur no shipping costs) and the value of the order subtotal (shipping is free for purchases over $50). To exercise the "shipping cost calculation" code, you would need to test a real item, not a digital download. To exercise the "free shipping discount" code, you would need to test a purchase over $50. To *thoroughly* test this functionality, you would also need to test purchases that are $50 or less—as well as ensure that shipping costs are not added for digital downloads.

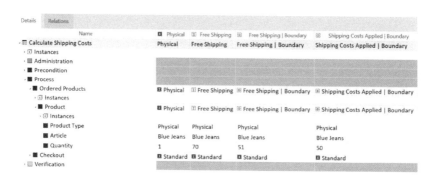

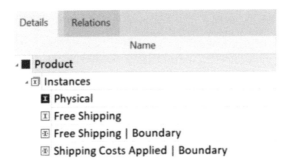

If your test design tool lets you specify relations, that should help you add the missing tests and avoid the meaningless ones. If not, you'll need to address this in a manual review. Nevertheless, the extremely efficient test suite that this process yields will save you tremendous time in the long run—throughout test execution, maintenance, test result review, and root cause analysis.

Tackling Your Top Risks

For the fastest path to high risk coverage, start with your highest-risk requirements, and then design "straight throughs" for each of them. Next, apply linear expansion to increase their risk coverage with minimal additional effort—while still maintaining a high degree of efficiency. The most critical straight throughs are great candidates for quick smoke testing, while the "linearly-expanded" versions are likely better-suited for more extensive regression test runs.

While building out your test suites, the "less is more" adage applies. You want just enough tests to cover your risks and help you track each test failure back to the responsible application logic. Anything beyond that will only increase your text execution time as well as your team's maintenance burden—so why waste time creating them in the first place?

Alternative Combinatorics Approaches

I strongly recommend the linear expansion test design approach based on the results I've seen it achieve. I believe it's the perfect balance of efficiency and specificity. However, there are a number of other combinatorial test design strategies you can choose from. The following sections provide a quick survey of how they all compare.

For all cases, assume the following simple scenario: an insurance calculator that considers 15 different attributes (gender, vehicle type, etc.), each of which can have 2 different instances (male/female, car/truck, etc.).

Linear Expansion

With the linear expansion strategy described above, you could cover the options with 16 tests. First, you would start off by defining a "straight through" or "happy path" with the attributes that achieve the greatest risk coverage. You then vary one attribute value for each test. Each test has a clear objective: one test checks the functionality for the female discount, one test checks the functionality for the heavy payload rate increase, etc. You end up with slightly more tests than the ultra-efficient orthogonal approach presented below, but the test increase is still linear—you don't end up with a combinatorial explosion of tests.

All Possible Combinations

If you decide to test all possible combinations, you will end up with a combinatorial explosion of tests: 32,768 tests! Since you're covering each and every possible combination, risk coverage is extremely high. However, this is just an extremely simple example, and the number of tests is already unmanageable. Few teams will have the resources to create, execute, review, and maintain all of these tests. Moreover, when a test fails, you can't instantly tell which corresponding attribute or instance is responsible for the failure. You'd have to review the outcomes of many of the 32,767 other tests to determine exactly what triggered the failure.

Pairwise (All Pairs)

Pairwise approaches aim to cover each pair of instances for all business-relevant attributes at least once. With a pairwise approach, you could use 20 tests to cover all 420 possible pairs. Here, you avoid the combinatorial explosion of test cases; instead, you get logarithmic growth in attributes and quadratic growth in instances. However, each test still does not have a unique test objective, which means that additional review is required to determine what a test failure really means.

Orthogonal/Each Choice

The orthogonal approach aims to cover each attribute at least once. You can achieve this with 2 test cases that cover 30 singles. This is the absolute minimum number of test cases you could have and still cover all 30 of the attributes. However, if a test failed, you'd have to run additional testing to determine exactly which attribute and instance triggered the failure.

In summary:

	Test cases required	Growth in test cases	Test precision	Root cause analysis
Linear Expansion	16 test cases cover 30 singles	Acceptable (Linear)	High	Easy
All possible combinations	32,768	Extreme	Low	Difficult
Pairwise	20 test cases cover 420 pairs	Acceptable (logarithmic)	Low	Difficult
Each choice (orthogonal)	2 test cases cover 30 singles	Minimal	Low	Difficult

CHAPTER 5

Automate Testing for Fast Feedback

To derive the greatest value from a carefully-crafted test design, you must ensure that the planned tests are executed as rapidly and as often as needed. In yesterday's waterfall development iterations, manual testing was often a viable—though costly—solution. The benefit of automation has always been evident. Yet, with labor arbitrage, the low cost of manual testing allowed it to remain prevalent for much longer than it should. With cost-effective manual testing options at their fingertips, organizations deferred initiatives to build and scale test automation.

Even 5 years ago, only 30% of enterprise software testing was performed fully "in house," and the vast majority of that testing was not automated.[9] Today, 97% of organizations are practicing Agile to some degree and 73% have active or planned DevOps initiatives.[10] With this fundamental shift, test automation reaches a tipping point. Test*ers* are expected to be embedded in the team and test*ing* is expected to be completed "in-sprint." With this fundamental shift, test automation reaches a tipping point.

Why does the shift to Agile and DevOps make test automation imperative?

[9] Capgemini, Sogeti, HP, "World Quality Report" 2014-2015 (https://www.capgemini.com/resources/world-quality-report-2014-15/).
[10] CollabNet VersionOne, "13th Annual State of Agile Report" 2019 (https://www.stateofagile.com/).

- **There's less time available to test:** Modern application development involves releasing increasingly complex and distributed applications on increasingly tight timelines. It's just not possible to complete the required scope and complexity of testing "in sprint" without careful test design and a high degree of automation. Manual test cycles take weeks. This doesn't align with today's cadences, where 2-week sprints and (at least) daily builds have become the norm—and the trend is now edging towards Continuous Delivery.

- **Teams expect continuous, near-instant feedback:** Agile and DevOps teams expect feedback to be delivered continuously throughout the release cycle. This just isn't possible with manual testing—even if you hire an entire army of manual testers (which would be exorbitantly expensive, by the way). Without fast feedback on how the latest changes impact core end-to-end transactions, accelerated delivery puts the user experience at risk with each and every release.

- **Business expectations are dramatically different:** As companies prioritize Digital Transformation initiatives, the old adage of "speed, cost, quality…pick two" no longer applies. Amidst pressure to stabilize (and even reduce) costs, IT leaders are now expected to deliver more innovative applications faster than ever. Today, everyone from the CEO down recognizes that skimping on quality inevitably leads to brand erosion as well as customer defection. In regulated industries, the repercussions of subpar quality are even more severe.

Most organizations already understand that test automation is essential for modern application delivery processes. They're just not sure how to make it a reality in an enterprise environment—without exorbitant overhead and massive disruption.

You can't really blame them. Although there's no shortage of test automation success stories floating around software testing conferences, webinars, and publications, they primarily feature developers and technical testers that 1) are focused on testing simple web UIs and 2) have had the luxury of building their applications and testing processes from the ground up in the past few years. Their stories are compelling—but not entirely relevant for the typical Global 2000 company with heterogeneous architectures, compliance requirements, and quality processes that have evolved slowly over decades.

Test Automation Reality vs. Target

Before diving deeper into test automation, let's clarify what we're talking about here. Many types of tests can (and should) be automated. For example:

- **Unit tests** that check a function or class (programming units) in isolation
- **Component tests** that check the interactions of several units in the context of the application
- **Functional validation tests** that determine whether a specific requirement is satisfied
- **End-to-end functional tests** that exercise "end-to-end" business transactions across multiple components and applications from the user perspective (UI or API layer)
- **Performance tests** that measure an application's reliability, scalability, and availability under load—at any of the above levels

This book focuses on functional validation and end-to-end functional tests. Yet, most reports of "test automation rates" include *all* types of test automation—including unit test automation, which is commonly practiced by developers (more on unit testing later, in Appendix B).

At Tricentis, we've found that companies initially report that they have automated around 18% of the end-to-end functional tests they have designed and added to their test suite. It's actually much lower when you consider how many tests are actually running on a regular basis. And, when you focus on Global 2000 enterprises, it drops even further to a dismal 8%.[11]

The World Quality Report, which is based on 1,600 interviews drawn primarily from companies with 10,000+ employees, also reports test automation rates below 20%:

"The level of automation of testing activities is still very low (between 14-18% for different activities). This low level of automation is the number-one bottleneck for maturing testing in enterprises." [12]

Whichever source you choose, the bottom line is the same: there's a huge gap between where we are and where we need to be.

Where should we be? Forrester Research reports that Continuous Testing requires test automation rates to be *much* higher: "As a rule of thumb, manual testing should account for less than 20% of the overall testing activity; automated testing should account for more than 80%."[13]

This leads to what I call "the Continuous Testing rainbow":

[11] Tricentis research conducted from 2015-2018.

[12] Capgemini, Sogeti, HPE, World Quality Report 2018-19, 2019 (https://www.capgemini.com/service/world-quality-report-2018-19/).

[13] Diego lo Giudice, The Forrester Wave: Modern Application Functional Test Automation Tools, 2016 (https://www.forrester.com/report/The+Forrester+Wave+Modern+Application+Functional+Test+Automation+Tools+Q4+2016/-/E-RES123866)

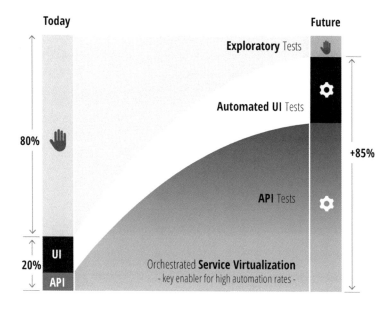

To enable Continuous Testing, automation rates need to exceed 85%. The only remaining manual tests should be exploratory tests, and the type of automation should shift as well. Automation should focus predominantly on the API or message level, requiring service virtualization to simulate the many dependent APIs and other components that are not continuously available or accessible for automated end-to-end testing. UI test automation will not vanish, but it will no longer be the focal point of automation.

Before exploring what's needed to reach this ideal state, let's take a look at why there's such a gap in the first place.

Why is Test Automation So Hard?

Many organizations have experimented with test automation: typically, automating some UI tests and integrating their execution into the Continuous Integration process. They achieve and celebrate small victories, but the process doesn't expand. In fact, it ultimately decays. Why? It usually boils down to roadblocks that fall into the following categories:

- Time and resources
- Complexity
- Trust
- Stakeholder alignment
- Scale

Time and Resources

Teams severely underestimate the time and resources required for sustainable test automation. Yes, getting some basic UI tests to run automatically is a great start. However, you also need to plan for the time and resources required to:

- Determine what to test and how to test it
- Establish a test framework that supports reuse and data-driven testing—both of which are essential for making automation sustainable over the long term
- Keep the broader test framework in sync with the constantly-evolving application
- Execute the test suite—especially if you're trying to frequently run a large, UI-heavy test suite
- Review and troubleshoot test failures—many of which are "false positives" (failures that don't indicate a problem with the application)
- Determine if each false positive stems from a test data issue, a test environment issue, or a "brittle" script (e.g., a test that's overly-sensitive to expected application changes, like dynamic name and date elements)
- Add, update, or extend tests as the application evolves; the more "bloated" your test suite is (e.g., with a high degree of redundancy and low level of reuse), the more difficult it will be to update

- Determine how to automate more advanced use cases and keep them running consistently in a Continuous Testing environment
- Review and interpret the mounting volume of test results

Complexity

It's one thing to automate a test for a simple "create" action in a web application (e.g., create a new account and complete a simple transaction from scratch). It's another to automate the most business-critical transactions, which typically pass through multiple technologies (mobile, APIs, SAP, mainframes, etc.) and require sophisticated setup and orchestration. To realistically assess the end-to-end user experience in a pre-production environment, you need to ensure that:

- Your testing resources understand how to automate tests across all the different technologies and connect data and results from one technology to another
- You have the stateful, secure, and compliant test data required to set up a realistic test as well as drive the test through a complex series of steps—each and every time the test is executed
- You have reliable, continuous, and cost-effective access to all the dependent systems that are required for your tests—including APIs, third-party applications, etc. that may be unstable, evolving, or accessible only at limited times

Trust

The most common complaint with test results is the overwhelming number of false positives that need to be reviewed and addressed. When you're just starting off with test automation, it might be feasible to handle the false positives. However, as your test suite grows and your test frequency increases, addressing false positives quickly becomes an insurmountable task.

Once you start ignoring false positives, you're on a slippery slope. Developers start assuming that *every* issue exposed by testing is a false positive—and testers need to work even harder to get critical issues addressed. Moreover, if stakeholders don't trust test results, they're not going to base go/no-go decisions on them.

Stakeholder Alignment

Back in Chapter 1, I said that Continuous Testing involves providing the right feedback to the right stakeholder at the right time. During the sprint, this might mean alerting the developers when a "small tweak" actually has a significant impact on the broader user experience. As the release approaches, it might mean helping the product owner understand what percentage of the application's risks are tested and passing. Yet, most teams focus on measuring non-actionable "counting" metrics, such as number of tests, that are hardly the right feedback for any stakeholder—at any time.[14]

Scale

Most test automation initiatives start with the highest-performing teams in the organization. It makes sense. They're typically the most eager to take on new challenges—and the best prepared to drive the new project to success. Chances are that if you look at any organization with pockets of test automation success, you will find that it's achieved by their elite teams. This is a great start…but it must scale throughout the entire organization to achieve the speed, accuracy, and visibility required for today's accelerated, highly-automated software delivery processes.

Bridging the Gap

How can everyone—including mature companies with complex systems—bridge the gap to achieve the required level of automation, reaching the ideal >85% test automation rate at the end of the Continuous Testing rainbow (shown on page 47)? The fast answer is: it depends.

---

[14] Forrester Research, Forrester Research on DevOps Quality Metrics that Matter, 2019 (https://www.tricentis.com/devops-quality-metrics)

Next, I'll outline the top four strategies that have helped many Global 2000 organizations finally break through the "test automation" barrier after many years of trying:

1. Simplify automation across the technology stack
2. End the test maintenance nightmare
3. Shift to API testing whenever feasible
4. Choose the right tool(s) for your needs

As you read through them, it's critical to recognize that there is no single "right approach" that suits every department in every organization. For each of the top strategies, I'll point out some considerations that could impact its importance in your organization.

Let's look at each of these four strategies in turn.

Simplify Automation Across the Technology Stack

Traditional approaches to test automation rely on script-based technologies. Before automation can begin, a test automation framework must be developed. Once the framework is finally implemented, tested, and debugged, test scripts can be added to leverage that framework. As the application evolves, these test scripts—and the test automation framework itself—also need to be reviewed, potentially updated, and debugged.

Often, significant resources are required to ramp up test automation for just a single technology (e.g., a web UI or mobile interface). This could include training existing testers on the specific scripting approach you've selected, reallocating development resources to testing, and/or hiring new resources who have already mastered that specific approach to script-based test automation. Even testers who are well-versed in scripting find that building, scaling, and maintaining test automation is a tedious, time-consuming task. It's often a distraction from testers' core competency: applying their domain expertise to identify issues that compromise the user experience and introduce business risks.

If you have a heterogeneous application stack to test (for example, packaged applications such as SAP/Salesforce/ServiceNow/Oracle EBS + APIs+ ESBs + mainframes + databases + web and mobile front ends), multiple frameworks will need to be learned, built, and linked in order to automate an end-to-end test case. Selenium—by far the most popular of all modern test automation frameworks—focuses exclusively on automating web UIs. For mobile UIs, you need Appium, a similar (but not identical) framework. Also testing APIs, data, packaged applications, and so forth? That means that even more tools and frameworks need to be acquired, configured, learned, and linked together.

Now, let's take a step back and remember the ultimate goal of automation: **speeding up your testing** so that the expected testing can be performed as rapidly and frequently as needed. To achieve this, you need a test automation approach that enables *your* testing team to rapidly build end-to-end test automation for *your* applications. If your testing team is made up of scripting experts and your application is a simple web app, Selenium or free Selenium-based tools might be a good fit for you. If your team is dominated by business domain experts and your applications rely on a broader mix of technologies, you're probably going to need a test automation approach that simplifies the complexity of testing enterprise apps and enables the typical enterprise user to be productive with a minimal learning curve.

You might find that different parts of your organization prefer different approaches (e.g., the teams working on customer-facing interfaces such as mobile apps might not want to use the same testing approach as the teams working on back-end processing systems). That's fine—just ensure that all approaches and technologies are connected in a way that fosters collaboration and reuse while providing centralized visibility.

> **Key Considerations:** This strategy is most important for testing in complex enterprise environments that involve multiple technologies—for example, packaged apps (SAP, Salesforce, etc.) + APIs + ESBs + web + mobile. The more different interfaces you are testing, the more you should prioritize this. If you are a small team testing a single interface, this probably is not an issue for you.

End the Test Maintenance Nightmare

Maintenance is the first—and most formidable—of what I call *the three nightmares of test automation*. (The other two nightmares are test data and test environments—both of which are covered in the next chapter).

If your tests are difficult to maintain, your test automation initiative **will** fail. If you're truly committed to keeping brittle scripts in check, you'll sink a tremendous amount of time and resources into test maintenance—eroding the time savings promised by test automation and making testing (once again) a process bottleneck. If you're not 100% committed to maintaining tests, your test results will be riddled by false positives (and false negatives) to the point that test results are no longer trusted.

Maintenance issues stem from two core problems:
1. Tests that are unstable
2. Tests that are difficult to update

The key to resolving the instability issue is to find a more robust way of expressing the test. If your automated test starts failing when your application hasn't changed, you've got a stability problem on your hands. There are a number of technical solutions for addressing this when it occurs (e.g., using more stable identifiers). These strategies are important to master. However, it's also essential to consider test stability from the very start of your test automation initiative. When you're evaluating test automation solutions, pay close attention to how the tool responds to acceptable/expected variations and how much work is required to keep the tool in sync with the evolving application. Also, recognize that even the most stable tests can encounter issues if they're being run with inappropriate test data or in unstable or incomplete test environments. I'll cover that in the next chapter.

To address the updating issue, modularity and reuse are key. You can't afford to update every impacted test every time that the development team improves or extends existing functionality (which can now be daily, hourly, or even more frequently). For the efficiency and "leanness" required to keep testing in sync with development, tests should be built from easily-updatable modules that are reused across the test suite. When business processes change, you want to be able to update a single module and have impacted tests automatically synchronized.

Effective test case design (covered in Chapter 4) is essential for getting—and keeping—both of these potential issues under control. As I said then, "less is more": you want just enough tests so that when a test fails, you know exactly what application functionality to investigate. With test case design methodologies like linear expansion, the team knows exactly which tests need to be added as the application evolves. This saves time in both the short term (fewer tests need to be added in each sprint) and the long term (fewer tests fail and require maintenance over the application's lifespan). If you have a combinatorial explosion of tests, ensuring test suite stability and keeping tests up-to-date will inevitably be a Sisyphean task—no matter what approach and technologies you use.

Key Considerations: This strategy is most important for 1) teams hoping to achieve high levels of automation and 2) teams working with actively-evolving applications. If you're trying to automate a few basic tests for a relatively static application, you might have sufficient time and resources to address the required maintenance. However, the more test automation you build and/or the more frequently the application is changing, the sooner test maintenance will become a prohibitive nightmare. Also, fast-growing and high-turnover teams are more vulnerable to "test bloat": an accumulation of redundant tests that add no value in terms of risk coverage but still require resources to execute, review, and update. Focusing on reuse and applying the test design strategies outlined in Chapter 4 will keep bloat to a minimum.

Shift to API Testing

Today, UI testing accounts for the vast majority of functional test automation—with only a small fraction of testing being conducted at the API level. However, a second look at the Continuous Testing Rainbow shows that we need to reach a state that's essentially reversed:

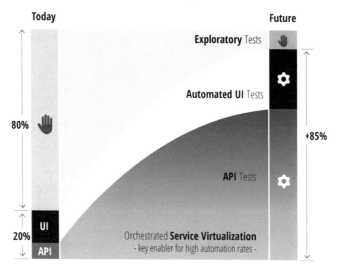

Why? API testing is widely recognized as being much more suitable for modern development processes because:

- Since APIs (the "transaction layer") are considered the most stable interface to the system under test, API tests are less brittle and easier to maintain than UI tests

- API tests can be implemented and executed earlier in each sprint than UI tests[15]

- API tests can often verify detailed "under-the-hood" functionality that lies beyond the scope of UI tests

- API tests are much faster to execute and are thus suitable for checking whether each new build impacts the existing user experience

In fact, Tricentis' recent studies have quantified some of the key advantages of using API testing versus UI test automation:[16]

Task	UI Test Automation	API Testing	Factor
Set-up	100%	25%	4x
Maintenance	100%	16%	6x
Runtime	100%	<1%	100+ x
Timing	**Regressive**	*Progressive*	

This leads to my recommended take on the test pyramid:

---

[15] Moreover, with service virtualization simulating APIs that are not yet completed, you can "shift left" testing even further with a TDD approach. Service virtualization is covered in the next chapter.

[16] Tricentis research conducted from 2015-2018 at Global 2000 companies—primarily across finance, insurance, telecom, retail, and energy sectors.

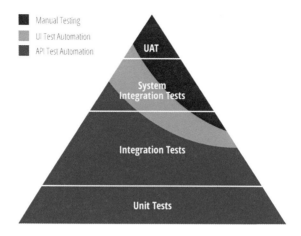

The red tip of the pyramid indicates the role that manual testing (typically via exploratory testing—more on this in the next chapter) is best suited to play in modern development processes. The green band represents what we've found to be the "sweet spot" for UI test automation. The vast majority of the triangle is covered by API testing, which builds upon development-level unit testing.

Your "Test Pyramid" Might Be a Diamond

Over time, the test pyramid actually erodes into a diamond. Appendix B explains why the bottom falls out, making the pyramid unstable. It also shares what you can do to prevent this.

From a practical standpoint, how do you determine what should be tested at the API layer and which tests should remain at the UI layer? The general rule of thumb is that you want to be as close to the business logic as possible. If the business logic is exposed via an API, use API tests to validate that logic. Then, reserve UI testing for situations when you want to validate the presence/location of UI elements or functionality that is expected to vary across devices, browsers, etc. In parallel, developers can (and should) be testing the API's underlying code at the unit level to expose implementation errors as soon as they are introduced.

Key considerations: Obviously, if the functionality you're tasked with testing is not exposed via APIs, this is not a viable strategy for you. For example, if you're testing an SAP application that's not leveraging APIs, API testing simply isn't an option. You need to ensure test repeatability and stability in another way.

Choose the Right Tool(s) for Your Needs

There's no shortage of open source and free test automation tools on the market. If you're introducing test automation into a small team testing a single web or mobile interface—or isolated APIs— you can very likely find a free tool that will help you get started and achieve some impressive test automation gains.

On the other hand, if you're a large organization testing business transactions that pass through SAP, APIs, mainframes, web, mobile, and more, you need a test automation tool that will simplify testing across all these technologies—in a way that enables team members to efficiently reuse and build upon each other's work.

To help you compare commercial and/or open source testing tools based on your top criteria, Tricentis prepared a fully-customizable testing tool comparison matrix. You can enter your own scoring for each tool, specify how you want to weight various criteria, and even factor in additional criteria that are important to your team/organization. You can download it at https://www.tricentis.com/CTbook.

However, before you focus on selecting a tool, consider this: the greatest mistake that organizations make with test automation initiatives is thinking that acquiring a test automation tool is the most important step in adopting test automation. Unfortunately, it's not that easy. No matter which tool you select, it's absolutely essential that you regard it as just one component of a much broader transformation that touches process, people, and technologies.

> **Key considerations:** Cost is undeniably a factor in every tool acquisition decision. Be sure to consider the *total cost of ownership*—including what's required to train and ramp up your existing resources (or hire additional ones), build test frameworks, build and maintain tests, and so on. Also, recognize that it's fully feasible (and often valuable) to have different teams using different tools. A small team creating a mobile app for your annual corporate event does not need to use the same tool as the team testing how your SAP-based business critical transactions are impacted by frequent upgrades. "Single pane of glass" reporting provides centralized visibility while allowing each team and division to choose the best tool for their needs.

Model-Based Test Automation: The Fast Track to Sustainable Test Automation

All the strategies I've presented throughout this chapter are applicable across test automation technologies. However, I'd be remiss if I didn't introduce Model-Based Test Automation and explain why I firmly believe it's the perfect solution for enterprises ramping up test automation. This is a topic I'm extremely passionate about. For me, it's personal.

Almost two decades ago, I joined forces with three colleagues to provide IT-related services for insurance companies across Austria. We performed a small amount of software development, but our primary focus was software quality assurance. In 1999, one of the world's largest insurers asked our company to help them adopt test automation. After trying out all the tools on the market, we settled on SQA Robot (later acquired by Rational, then IBM). However, after a 10-day honeymoon phase, we fell right into the maintenance trap that still afflicts test automation efforts today. Creating test cases was simple (for someone with my technical background, at least), but maintaining them was a nightmare that required a significant amount of time and technical programming. It was immediately clear that the client's testing team could never keep up with all the maintenance required, so I decided to write an abstraction layer.

This approach to test automation was a success from the start, and the client rapidly ramped up test automation. Over the next few years, we saw an increasing demand for this tool across enterprise clients throughout Austria and Switzerland. After their initial test automation initiatives failed (they were always caught in the maintenance trap), the companies reached out to us—seeking a different, more sustainable approach to test automation.

By 2003, we recognized that there was a real need for this particular "business abstraction layer" testing technology. We also realized that it could thrive on the software testing market—beyond the scope of the IT services we were personally delivering. To make a long story short, we dedicated tremendous research and development resources into advancing this technology and pairing it with a modern automation engine. Today, the outcome of all this R&D is known as "Model-Based Test Automation"—the core technology that Tricentis is recognized for.

What is Model-Based Test Automation?

Model-Based Test Automation (MBTA) is architected to enable anyone from developers to business experts to contribute to test automation—while eliminating the maintenance burden that erodes most test automation initiatives. Instead of programming a test automation framework, you scan the application's UI or API to create a business-readable automation model.

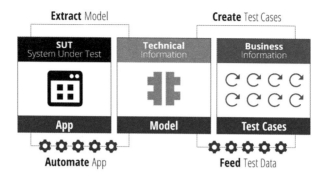

These models provide Lego-like "building blocks" that can be combined and reused to create your tests. If your application changes (e.g., a field is added or removed), you just update the model, and the change is automatically propagated to all impacted tests.

The key principles of the Model-Based Test Automation approach are:

Abstract the Automation Details Into Business-Readable Modules

Instead of programming a test automation framework, you scan the application's interface (UI or API) to create an automation model. This automation model contains the information needed to exercise the application under test. One "module" is created to locate and interact with each of the UI elements, API operations, etc. that are relevant for your testing.

Each module is represented in human-readable language. For example, assume you are trying to automate a checkbox like this:

☐ * Yes, I agree to receive periodic communications, emails and promotional materials from Tricentis related to products and services and can unsubscribe at any time.

A traditional automation script might represent it as something like

```
CheckBox Click,
"/usr/cntlCONTAINER/shellcont/shell[2]/chbx[1,3]"
```

With Model-Based Test Automation, it would be represented as something like:

Name	Value	ActionMode	DataType
⟳ Opt in to Mail Updates			
☑ Accept Terms	True	Input	String

In terms of emphasizing abstraction and reuse, it's actually a lot like object-oriented programming. Being able to work at this high level makes the test creation process much faster and less error-prone.

Separate the Automation Details, Test Logic, and Test Data

With a clear separation between automation details (e.g., "steering"), test logic, and test data, the impact of each change is isolated to a single component. The test logic and test data are injected into the automation model at runtime—guaranteeing that tests never use old versions of test data or access outdated technical definitions.

For example, if your loan approval service was reimplemented using a new back-end technology, your test cases wouldn't need to change at all. Only the automation details would be impacted. If you wanted to increase your risk coverage by validating more advanced use cases, you could test different test flows, conditions, and sequences without having to change any automation details. And if you needed to update your data set (e.g., to comply with data privacy regulations such as GDPR), you could achieve this without ever touching your automation details or test logic.

Maximize Reuse

Test cases are created by combining the modules (building blocks representing the various interface elements) into logical test scenario sequences. A single module can be used in any number of test cases. If the associated interface element later changes (for example, a new checkbox was added to your signup form), you only need to update the impacted module once. The change will automatically be propagated to all the test cases which use that module. Moreover, test logic is also reusable. Since the test logic is separate from the automation details, teams can reuse the same test logic across different interfaces or technologies (mobile, cross-browser, etc.). Likewise, the same data can also be applied across different technologies.

Enable Standardization and Flexibility

Modules are built and used in a standard way whether they represent SAP, mobile, APIs, custom applications, etc. This means that once a tester is familiar with Model-Based Test Automation for one technology (say, web UI test automation), it's extremely simple for that same person to apply the same concepts to all other technologies that need to be tested (for example, mobile, SAP, APIs, etc.) Moreover, since all different types of modules can be mixed and matched within a single test case, the test logic can easily mimic the flow of realistic end-to-end user transactions across today's highly-distributed systems.

Model-Based Test Automation for Agile and DevOps

I could go on and on about Model-Based Test Automation. For the purpose of this book, let's focus on how it helps Global 2000 companies achieve the fast, flexible, and sustainable test automation required for Agile and DevOps:

- Model-Based Test Automation ensures that the constant change typical of modern fast-paced development processes does not cause a test maintenance nightmare.

- Testers are empowered to complete the expected level of testing within the extremely compressed test windows that are fast-becoming the norm.

- Flaky tests don't block builds when testing is used as a quality gate during Continuous Integration and throughout DevOps pipelines.

- Since programming/scripting experience is not required, you don't need to wait on programming resources to assist with test automation. Testers of all levels, business analysts, and other subject matter experts can contribute to the test automation effort.

In a sense, this is the low-code/no-code software development approach applied to software testing. Organizations have already recognized that low-code/no-code development is an efficient way to satisfy the relentless demand for more software, faster. It helps enterprise organizations deliver software as efficiently as startups by maximizing reuse and minimizing the need for hand-coding. Freed from the complexities of low-level implementation details, teams can move fast and focus on the high-level, strategic work that adds business value. This is exactly what Model-Based Test Automation aims to enable.

CHAPTER 6

Completing the Continuous Testing Puzzle

Up to this point, we've covered how to:

- Prioritize requirements by risk—so you can test the top business risks first
- Design tests that cover your risks as efficiently as possible
- Automate tests rapidly, with minimal maintenance
- See the risk impact of your test failures
- Identify critical "blind spots" that are not yet tested

By putting these strategies into practice, you'll make great strides towards the rapid, business-focused feedback critical for Agile and DevOps. But more is needed to provide this feedback continuously, and to ensure that it's available for your advanced use cases as well as your basic ones. This is where practices like test data management and service virtualization come into play.

Moreover, while functional test automation is a core component of Continuous Testing, it's just one component. Of course, we need to know if a certain series of inputs and actions produces the expected results.

But what if the functionality is so slow—or so frustrating to use—that impatient customers decide to try a competitor? Exploratory testing and load testing can help you realistically assess and optimize the end-users' experience with your application.

Test Data Management

Test data management (TDM) is one of the critical capabilities that helps an organization evolve automated tests to continuous tests. It's impossible to achieve a mature Continuous Testing process unless you have an effective, tightly-integrated way to create, manage, and provision the data required for your tests. A successful TDM strategy is required for both end-to-end regression testing as well as load testing (covered later in this chapter).

However, obtaining and applying appropriate test data has always been challenging. It's especially tricky when you're testing complex scenarios— for example, when an account must be in a certain state before you can exercise some core functionality, or when order status changes multiple times throughout the course of a single transaction. And the more frequently you run tests (think of testing integrated into CI), the more difficult it becomes to ensure that the tests have access to the necessary range of fresh, unexpired test data.

Today, data privacy regulations like GDPR are further complicating an already-complex situation by forcing companies to abandon the most common test data management approach: using test data extracted from production environments.

Let's look at each of these challenges—stateful test data and secure, compliant test data—in turn.

Stateful Test Data

One of the greatest challenges associated with test data management is setting up and manipulating stateful data. Stateful test data not only produces the specific application conditions that are required to set up a realistic test; it also enables you to drive the test through a complex series of steps.

For example, imagine you want to test the reversal of fraudulent charges on a credit card account. First, you'd need to get the account into the "state" where an account was created and had a history of charges. Then, the test would need to indicate that certain charges were fraudulent and reduce the amount due accordingly.

How do you achieve this? By registering the change of states in your test data management repository—where it can then be retrieved by the next step, which might cause another change of state, and so on and so on. Calling the same data reference (for instance, account status) at multiple points in a process might yield different results, based on what value is appropriate at each phase.

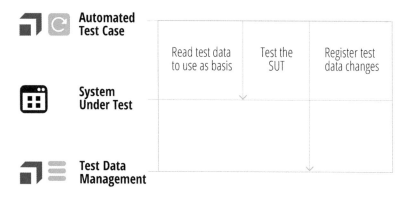

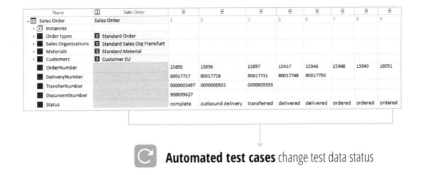

Name		Sales Order	≡	≡	≡	≡	≡	≡	≡	≡
⊿ ▦ Sales Order	Sales Order		1	2	3	5	6	7	8	9
▸ 🔢 Instances										
▸ ■ Order types	🔢 Standard Order									
▸ ■ Sales Organizations	🔢 Standard Sales Org Frankfurt									
▸ ■ Materials	🔢 Standard Material									
▸ ■ Customers	🔢 Customer EU									
■ OrderNumber			15895	15896	15897	15937	15946	15948	15949	16091
■ DeliveryNumber			80017717	80017718	80017731	80017748	80017750			
■ TransferNumber			0000005497	0000005503	0000005503					
■ DocumentNumber			900039627							
■ Status			complete	outbound delivery	transferred	delivered	delivered	ordered	ordered	ordered

C **Automated test cases** change test data status

Secure, GDPR-Compliant Test Data

There are two main ways to ensure that your test data complies with data privacy regulations like GDPR: masking production data and using synthetic test data.

Most organizations get their test data from production data because (1) it's available and (2) it's known to be realistic. However, GDPR means that production data can no longer be used as is if it contains any private data from any EU residents. Now, that data must be masked irreversibly and deterministically (i.e., the same way across all instances).

Another option is to synthetically generate the test data that you need. The fact that it's completely fake means that GDPR compliance becomes a nonissue. However, fake data can only get you so far. You can typically achieve high (though not perfect) risk coverage using synthetic test data alone. However, synthetic test data generation sometimes falls short when data objects with a long history are required for testing. For example, it might be difficult, or even impossible, to provide a 40-year life insurance contract that was signed 25 years ago. This type of legacy data typically needs to be extracted from production because it's not easily generated.

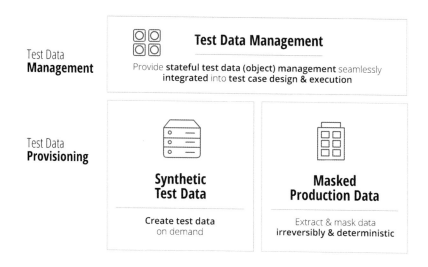

Fortunately, this limitation is narrow in scope. For example, Tricentis' research has found that in retail, synthetic test data can usually achieve 98% risk coverage. The coverage for telecoms is also high: 96%. With insurance and banks, it's a little lower, but still greater than 90%.[17]

Ultimately, you'll want to use both masked production data and synthetically-generated test data to address your various testing needs:

- **Masked production data** provides easy access to realistic test data. Extracting data from production and then masking it to meet GDPR privacy requirements can be a fast way to cover your most common use cases.
- **Synthetically-generated data** enables broader coverage and negative testing. It lets you simulate data types and ranges that might be difficult to find in production data.

My recommendation is to use synthetically-generated test data as much as possible, then fill in the gaps with masked production data. You'll dramatically reduce the amount of test data that falls under the scope of GDPR.

---

[17] Tricentis research conducted from 2015-2018 at Global 2000 companies—primarily across finance, insurance, telecom, retail, and energy sectors.

DevOps Toolchain Integration

Modern development teams are adopting a diverse assortment of tools to automate and optimize the software delivery pipeline. In response, today's toolchains now include best-of-breed tools that span numerous capabilities, product vendors, and team roles. The more effectively these tools integrate and interact, the more effectively team members can work and collaborate.

Tightly integrating testing activities with a best-of-breed DevOps toolchain fosters efficiency and collaboration. Integration with the organization's CI systems of choice is essential for making testing a seamless part of the delivery pipeline. You can directly integrate any modern testing platform into CI tools, or you can connect to a dedicated test management platform that orchestrates execution along with test management, tracking, and reporting. Additionally, technology to accelerate test execution (e.g., via distributed execution, fault recovery, etc.) can help you get more testing completed in the available time.

Service Virtualization

Shortly after you build your initial automated test suite and start executing it regularly—potentially as part of a CI effort—your dependencies are likely to create a roadblock. Your tests will expect the application's dependent system components (APIs, third-party applications, etc.) to be available in the test environment during every execution. However, with complex enterprise systems, at least some of the many required dependencies are probably incomplete, unavailable, or operating incorrectly at the time of test execution. Some might have changed versions, and others might be using inaccurate or expired test data. The result is timeouts, incomplete tests, false positives, and inaccurate results—preventing you from delivering the fast quality feedback expected with test automation.

Service virtualization can help you get past these roadblocks and increase test automation rates.

What Is Service Virtualization?

Service virtualization is a simulation technology that lets you automatically execute tests, even when the AUT's dependent system components (APIs, third-party applications, etc.) cannot be properly accessed or configured for testing. By simulating these dependencies, you can ensure that your tests will encounter the appropriate dependency behavior and data every time they execute.

Service virtualization is commonly used when integration tests or end-to-end tests need to interact with dependent system components that are:

- Unreliable, evolving, or not yet completed
- Beyond your scope of control (e.g., operated by another company or division)
- Available for testing only in a limited capacity or at inconvenient times
- Challenging to provision or configure in a test environment
- Simultaneously needed by different teams with varied test data set-ups and other requirements
- Too restricted or costly to use for automated regression testing

Stabilizing Automated Tests

For automated tests to execute successfully, all the dependent systems must be available with the appropriate configuration, functionality, and test data—all at the same time, every time the automated test suite executes. This is a tremendous challenge.

When an automated test suite's execution is impeded by timeouts, incomplete tests, false positives, or other testing problems, it's often a symptom

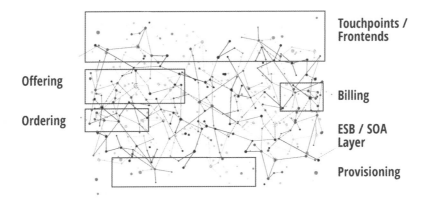

Touchpoints / Frontends

Offering

Ordering

Billing

ESB / SOA Layer

Provisioning

of test environment stability issues. With service virtualization, you can stabilize access to dependent systems so that tests can execute completely, reliably, and continuously.

For example, assume that you need to execute an end-to-end test that interacts with an order processing system beyond your immediate control. However, that order management system is continually being upgraded with new functionality that's irrelevant to your tests. As a result of those frequent updates, that dependency is often unavailable or unstable.

If you use service virtualization to simulate the small sliver of behavior and data that's required to execute your tests, you eliminate the risk of dependency issues interfering with your automated test execution. The more your tests are isolated from the various dependencies they interact with, the greater the chance that your automated test execution will proceed as planned.

By simulating dependencies in this manner, you can also trust that your test failures stem from issues with your AUT, not problems with your test environment; and you can reliably re-create the test environment for defect reproduction or bug fix validation.

Automating Complex Test Scenarios

Once the initial automated test suite is running like a fine-tuned machine, the next goal is often to automate more advanced test cases. However, it can be considerably more challenging to eliminate dependency issues for complex scenarios that involve stateful transactions than for simpler test cases that simply search for data or add a new object.

For example, assume you are responsible for testing an account management system that interacts with a CRM beyond your scope of control. You might need to test a scenario that:

1. Loads an existing customer account and checks that pricing details are appropriate for their current address
2. Pays the customer's full account balance based on their current address
3. Changes the customer's address to a more expensive area
4. Reloads the customer's account details and validates that the pricing details are updated appropriately based on the new address
5. Validates that a) an additional amount due is added to the customer's account, and b) the account status changes from "paid in full" to "payment due"

With traditional service virtualization approaches, it would be difficult to simulate the dependencies involved in executing this test case. But this is where orchestrated service virtualization—a special type of testing that is driven from the perspective of the test—shines.

Here, it lets you accurately simulate the various stateful customer account updates so that you can test without having to actually interact with (or configure) the back-end CRM system. It can also eliminate any associated system delays (e.g., waiting for the address update to enter the system and the pricing details to update), which could otherwise introduce a bottleneck into the automated testing process.

Basic service virtualization scenario:

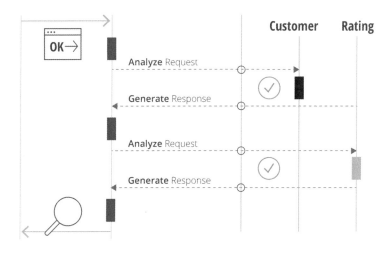

Advanced service virtualization scenario:

Orchestrated service virtualization is sometimes called test-driven service virtualization because it focuses on simulation from the perspective of the test and places the tester at the center of service virtualization asset creation and management.

Service virtualization also provides a simple way to test how your AUT behaves against edge cases and error conditions that would be difficult to configure in a staged test environment. For example, assume that your account management system interacts with multiple dependent systems (a CRM, location system, and order processing system), and you want to automate tests that validate how your AUT reacts when different combinations of dependent systems are down, delayed, or behaving incorrectly. Or, assume that you want to automate a test that validates how your AUT reacts when its expected messages are sent or received in an incorrect order. Service virtualization helps you simulate these conditions so that you can automate the broad range of tests required to effectively cover your risks.

Ensuring Fast, Quality Test Feedback

If you can guarantee that all the dependent systems associated with your end-to-end tests will always be available, operating correctly, and configured with appropriate test data every time your automated tests execute, you might not need service virtualization. But for everyone else, it's vital for achieving the sustainable, scalable test automation required for Continuous Testing, Agile, and DevOps.

Providing the team with fast quality feedback is one of the top goals of test automation. The goal of service virtualization is to ensure that test environment issues don't impact the speed, accuracy, or completeness of that feedback—so you can satisfy business expectations for quality at speed.

Exploratory Testing

Test automation is perfect for repeatedly checking whether incremental application changes break your existing functionality. However, test automation falls short for determining if new functionality truly meets expectations. Does it address the business needs behind the user story? Does it do so in a way that's easy to use, resource-efficient, reliable, and consistent with the rest of your application?

The specification-based testing I've been focusing on throughout this book checks whether expected paths through user stories are free of predictable issues. But what about dangers lurking beyond the primary paths?

This is where exploratory testing comes in. Exploratory testing promotes the creative testing required to answer these and other critical questions about the viability of new functionality. Here are three reasons exploratory testing is such a great complement to test automation in Agile and DevOps processes.

Rapidly Expose Issues—Including Those That Might Escape Other Testing Methods

By scouting and exploring new product territories from various perspectives—without extensive planning or automation efforts—exploratory testing rapidly exposes many severe defects in a short period of time. Since it leverages human intelligence, exploratory testing gives you a broader and deeper view than any automated test could. For example, an automated test could tell you if a UI element worked properly, but it could not determine if that UI element was confusing to the end user. Even if exhaustive automated testing was feasible—which it's not in compressed Agile sprints—such issues would still evade it. Since exploratory testing encourages branching and, well, exploration of different stories and ideas, it uncovers different issues than structured, predefined testing typically does.

Specification-based testing is always critical for determining whether a user story is "done done." Of course, you want to know whether the new functionality actually does what it is expected to do. But a clean bill of health on functional testing doesn't mean that the functionality won't negatively impact the end user and maybe even drive them away from your application. Understandability, usability, accessibility and other "-ities" are beyond the scope of automated functional testing but are often imperative for ensuring a positive user experience.

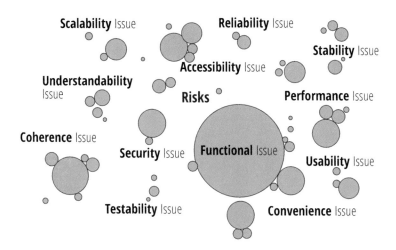

Moreover, there is often a gap between the functionality that's specified and the functionality that's actually implemented. Sometimes functionality is specified but not implemented. Specification-based testing can catch this. However, sometimes teams implement functionality that's not specified—often, as the result of a developer misinterpreting the requirements.

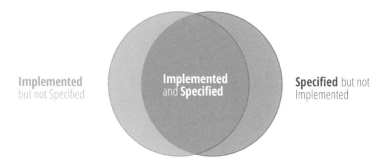

Tests that strictly follow the specification will not venture into this area of the actual product. They might not even detect that the implementation went beyond the specification. Exploratory testing, on the other hand, is likely to discover the unspecified-but-implemented functionality as well as expose any critical issues within that area.

In other words, specification-based testing helps you check if expected paths are free of predictable issues. Exploratory testing helps you discover what dangers might be lurking beyond the primary paths.

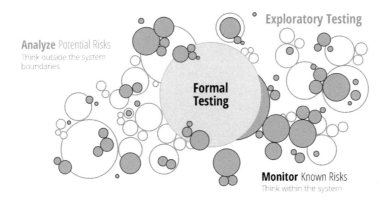

Facilitate Cross-Functional Team Collaboration to Expose More Types of Defects

With exploratory testing, a diverse group of people—from developers, to product owners, to UX designers, to business analysts, to technical writers, to support engineers—can all contribute to the quality effort since no specialized test automation or scripting knowledge is required. All these different people each bring different specialties and different perspectives to the table.

With a larger and more diverse group examining the application, you not only complete more testing in less time—you also expose a broader variety of issues and reduce the risk that a critical issue goes unnoticed. There's never enough time or resources to test absolutely everything.

However, if you perform exploratory testing from many different perspectives, you can get greater risk reduction from whatever time and resources you can dedicate to testing.

Find Issues Before Automated Testing

Exploratory testing is perfect for performing a quick sanity check on new functionality and its most prominent impacts across the application. It helps you rapidly identify the big blockers soon after they're introduced—enabling the team to "fail fast" before any test automation is implemented. If you use an exploratory testing tool to automatically record and document your efforts, any defects found are easily reproducible.

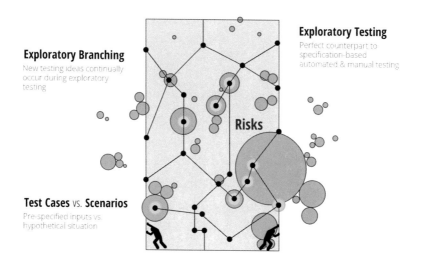

Exploratory Branching
New testing ideas continually occur during exploratory testing

Exploratory Testing
Perfect counterpart to specification-based automated & manual testing

Risks

Test Cases vs. **Scenarios**
Pre-specified inputs vs. hypothetical situation

Note that I'm *not* suggesting that exploratory testing is a substitute for automated testing. You still need an automated regression test suite to reliably determine if changes compromise your existing functionality. The scope of what you can cover with exploratory testing is a drop in the bucket compared to what you can check with automated testing. Rather, I'm trying to emphasize that exploratory testing can be a great way to uncover some critical issues even before you're ready for test automation.

Load Testing

Today's developers and testers don't have the time (or desire) to wrestle with all the technical details required to get traditional load tests working correctly and keep brittle load tests in sync with the rapidly evolving application.

The traditional way of approaching load testing is by scripting at the protocol level (e.g., HTTP). This includes load testing with open source tools such as JMeter and Gatling, as well as legacy commercial tools such as LoadRunner. Although simulating load at the protocol level has the advantage of being able to generate large concurrent load from a single resource, that power comes at a cost. The learning curve is steep, and the complexity is easily underestimated.

Why Load Testing is (Traditionally) Such a Pain

The main culprit for this complexity is JavaScript. In 2011, there was usually less than 100 KB of JavaScript per page, which spurred around 50 or fewer HTTP requests. Now, that's doubled: We see an average of 200 KB of JavaScript per page, and this gives us more than 100 requests per page.

For example, just one click on an Amazon.com page triggers something like 163 HTTP requests processed asynchronously after page load. You also find things such as dynamic parsing and execution of JavaScript, the browser cache being seeded with static assets and calls to content delivery networks. And the next time the same element is clicked, it might generate 161 requests…or 164…or 165. There will be small differences each time.

When you start building your load test simulation model, this will quickly translate into thousands of protocol-level requests that you need to faithfully record and then manipulate into a working script. You must review the request and response data, perform some cleanup and extract relevant information to realistically simulate user interactions at a business level. You can't just think like a user; you also must think like the browser.

You need to consider all the other functions that the browser is automatically handling for you, and figure out how you're going to compensate for that in your load test script. Session handling, cookie header management, authentication, caching, dynamic script parsing and execution, taking information from a response and using it in future requests ... all of this needs to be handled by your workload model and script if you want to successfully generate realistic load. Basically, you become responsible for doing whatever is needed to fill the gap between the technical and business level. This requires both time and technical specialization.

The Future of Load Testing is BLU
To sum up the challenge here: modern web applications are increasingly

difficult to simulate at the protocol level. This raises the question: Why not shift from the protocol level to the browser level—especially if the user's experience via the browser is what you ultimately want to measure and improve in order to advance the business' Digital Transformation initiatives?

When you're working at the browser level, one business action translates to maybe two automation commands in a browser as compared to tens, if not hundreds, of requests at the protocol level. Browser-level functions such as cache, cookie, and authentication/session management work without intervention.

There are a number of ways to simulate traffic at the browser-level: Selenium is currently the most popular, but there are a number of cross-browser testing tools available—some of which let you test without getting into scripting.

However, historically, it just wasn't feasible to run these tools at the scale needed for load testing. In 2011, if you wanted to launch 50,000 browsers with Selenium, you would have needed around 25,000 servers to provide the infrastructure. Moreover, it would have been prohibitively expensive and time-consuming to provision the necessary infrastructure.

Today, with the prominent availability of the cloud and containers, the concept of browser-based load testing is finally feasible. Suddenly, generating a load of 50,000 browsers is a lot more achievable—especially when the cloud can now give you access to thousands of load generators that can be up and running in minutes. Instead of having to wait for expensive performance test labs to get approved and set up, you can get going instantly at an infrastructure cost of just cents per hour. Instead of wrestling with 163 HTTP requests to test a simple user action, you just simulate one browser-level click—which is obviously much easier to define and maintain. Consider the number of clicks and actions in your average user transaction, and the time/effort savings add up rather quickly.

Fast feedback on performance is no longer just a pipe dream.

You can use open source technology like Flood Element to capture the action in a simple, easily maintainable script. Or, if you prefer a "low-code/no-code" approach, you can capture your test scenarios as scriptless functional tests, then use those same tests to drive both load testing and functional testing.

By reducing the complexity traditionally associated with load testing, BLU load testing gives developers and testers a fast, feasible way to get immediate feedback on how code changes impact performance. It's designed to help people who are not professional performance testers quickly create load tests that can be run continuously within a CI/CD process—with minimal maintenance.

Test Impact Analysis

In the spirit of "failing fast," teams want CI to provide feedback on their latest updates as soon as possible. CI test results are the primary barometer that developers use to determine whether it's safe to move on to the next development task, or if they inadvertently broke functionality that users have grown to rely on.

With more extensive and effective regression testing during CI, you're much more likely to spot critical problems as soon as they're introduced—which is when they're fastest, easiest, and cheapest to fix. However, given the frequency of builds in most Agile processes, there's simply not much time available for test execution. Developers expect feedback in a matter of minutes, but most regression test suites—especially in Global 2000 organizations—take hours (or days!) to execute. This seems to force a trade-off: settle for sluggish CI or scale down testing.

Slow CI impacts productivity across all team members waiting to review, extend, document, and test the new functionality. The closer the end-of-sprint deadline, the more painful each minute of waiting seems. Of course, you can (and should) accelerate the process with parallel/distributed test execution and similar technologies. But ultimately, if you want to accelerate the execution of a large enterprise test suite, you will need to make some hard decisions about what tests *do not* need to be executed for each build.

If you apply the risk-based prioritization and test design methodologies discussed in Chapters 3 and 4, you probably already have a tight, powerful test suite. But what if you need to further streamline test execution within your CI? One approach is to use test impact analysis. This technique, as pioneered by Technical University Munich spinoff CQSE, rapidly exposes issues in code added/modified since the previous test run by applying two main principles:[18]

- **Correlate** all regression tests (even end-to-end regression tests) to code and **select** only the tests associated with the latest round of code changes. Why waste time executing tests that have no chance of uncovering defects in your new/modified code?

- **Order** those regression tests based on their likelihood of detecting a problem—and **prioritize** execution of the ones that are most likely to expose defects. If your builds are set to fail upon the first reported test case failure, you might as well reach that point as soon as possible.

This enables you to find the lion's share of defects in a fraction of the time it would otherwise take. In fact, studies show that this approach uncovers 80% of faulty builds in 1% of the total test execution time—and it uncovers 90% of faulty builds in 2% of the total test execution time.[19] *In other words, you can speed up testing 100X and still find most problems.* It's ideal for optimizing Continuous Testing.

---

[18] For more details on CQSE, see https://www.cqse.eu/en/

This new way to "fail fast" results in much tighter feedback loops—which means that failing builds get resolved sooner and working builds are delivered faster. It also accelerates Agile team velocity in a few other ways:

- Test < > code correlation makes it easier to determine where additional tests need to be added—and when sufficient code coverage has already been achieved.

- Test < > code correlation also streamlines the defect remediation process. Especially with end-to-end tests, finding the code responsible for a test failure can be like searching for a needle in a haystack. With this correlation, you get a very precise path from the test sequence detecting a problem to the code that's responsible for it.

- By squeezing more—and more effective—testing into a short period of time, you reduce the number of defects reported late in the process and after delivery. This ultimately results in less time wasted on bug fixes/rework, fewer mid-sprint interruptions, and more resources to focus on innovation.

Change Impact Analysis for SAP and Packaged Applications

If you're among the 90% of Global 2000 organizations who build business processes around SAP software and other packaged applications (e.g., Salesforce), impact analysis is even more critical.

Deploying changes or upgrades to packaged applications is risky business. Each change can impact your core business processes, as well as the system

---

[19] This study, performed by CQSE, analyzed both proprietary and open source code, and covered software written for business information systems as well as embedded systems.

integrations, custom code, security and governance, and user training that these processes rely on. With SAP and other vendors ramping up their upgrade pace, running your entire regression test suite after each update is no longer practical. Few teams have the required time/resources to do so— and, in many cases, the existing test suite does not even cover the impacted functionality.

Instead of trying to "test everything," you can use impact analysis to identify the specific objects impacted by a given change, then assess which of your existing tests should be run to test those objects—and what new tests need to be added. This can reduce testing scope by ~15-20%.

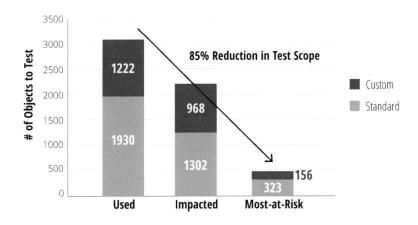

You can reduce the testing scope even further—by 85-95%—if you also apply the concept of risk. By incorporating usage information into your analysis, you can prioritize risk based on how frequently an object is used and its proximate dependency on a changed object. For example, a change on a payment UI used daily by thousands of customers obviously carries more risk than a change to a report that your organization never runs. This prioritization lets you really hone in on the set of tests that are most critical to run (or that need to be created in order to fill gaps).

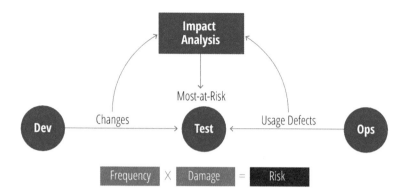

This drives a substantial reduction in effort—enabling you to focus your limited resources on the testing that matters most.

CHAPTER 7

Charting Your Path and Tracking Your Progress

So now you know the elements of Continuous Testing and—hopefully—you're ready to roll it out in your organization. Where do you begin?

If you've ever struggled to reach a destination without a pre-planned route, map, or trail, you know how frustrating a "trial-and-error" approach can be. Fortunately, you don't need to take that approach on your Continuous Testing journey. You can benefit from the lessons learned by others who have already taken that journey.

Continuous Testing Maturity Model

Based on Tricentis' experience guiding enterprise testing teams to optimized Continuous Testing, we have developed a Continuous Testing Maturity Model. We've found that this is the most efficient path to rolling out Continuous Testing in a way that's sustainable for the team—and valuable to IT leaders aiming to accelerate delivery without incurring unacceptable business risk.

You can use this model to assess where you stand today and understand what's needed to progress from one level to the next.

Level 1: The Typical Starting Point

At this initial level, the key metric is the number of test cases. All test cases are designed based on tester intuition. Testing is performed manually or is partially automated with a script-based approach (which results in a high rate of false positives that require constant maintenance). Testers must manually ensure test data suitability (e.g., by localizing and refining test data) and wait for dependencies to be provisioned in test environments. Any API testing is the domain of developers.

Anticipated efficiency gain: 1.3X

Level 2: Aligned

A risk assessment has been completed and risk coverage is now the key metric of test case definition and execution. Test automation still focuses on the UI, but now uses Model-Based Test Automation, which significantly reduces false positive rates and maintenance efforts. Since there is still no comprehensive test data management in place, automation primarily focuses on new data object creation rather than complex administrative use cases.

Anticipated efficiency gain: 3X

Level 3: Managed

Session-based exploratory testing is introduced to expose risks that specification-based testing cannot find (e.g., in functionality implemented beyond the boundaries of the specification). Additional test cases are defined via combinatorial test design methodologies such as linear expansion. If functionality is exposed via APIs, API testing is introduced at the tester level. UI testing, driven by Model-Based Test Automation, is extended in areas where API testing is not applicable or effective. Test automation is introduced into Continuous Integration through initial integrations with build and deployment tools.

Anticipated efficiency gain: 6X

Level 4: Mature

Test data management (TDM) now provides the test data needed to enable continuous, consistent test automation. Service virtualization ensures that testing can proceed even if dependent components are unstable or unavailable. The introduction of both TDM and service virtualization enables more sophisticated API testing, end-to-end testing, and continuous test execution. Tests can now be executed continuously as part of the software delivery pipeline—providing instant feedback on the business risk associated with the software release candidate.

Anticipated efficiency gain: >10X

Level 5: Optimized

Comprehensive test automation has been established and is supported by sophisticated, stateful service virtualization and test data generation/provisioning. Metrics are in place to monitor and continuously improve the effectiveness of the software testing process. Continuous Testing is fully integrated into Continuous Integration and the Continuous Delivery pipeline. The transformation into "DevTestOps" via Process, People and Product is achieved.

Anticipated efficiency gain: >20X

One Company's Path to Continuous Testing

To help you envision how this plays out in the real world, I want to share one organization's journey to comprehensive Continuous Testing. I've also collected videos of many QA leaders sharing their organizations' paths to Continuous Testing so you can gain insight into additional approaches and get a feel for how successful paths tend to vary.[20]

For this example, consider the path of a leading provider of core banking solutions. Banks across 100+ countries, serving over 1.95 billion customers, rely on their software to accelerate growth and improve customer service in an increasingly competitive banking market. They recently accelerated development speed 50%-66%+ with a scaled Agile (SAFe) initiative. At that point, testing emerged as the new process bottleneck: an expensive activity that was blamed for impeding innovation.

To transform their quality process for Agile delivery speeds, their quality leaders applied the principles described in this book. The main goals of

---

[20] For links, see https://www.tricentis.com/CTbook

this transformation were to complete testing faster, keep tests in sync with rapid application changes, and deliver the near-instant continuous quality feedback that the Agile development teams started to expect.

From Manual to Automated Testing

Like the vast majority of enterprise organizations, this company's quality process was dominated by manual testing and also included limited (largely abandoned) attempts at UI test automation. They had access to a legacy script-based test automation tool for over 10 years, but UI-based test automation scripts required constant rework and 50-75% of their testing resources were consumed by test script maintenance. Their library of 100K+ test cases had grown unmanageable. It was slow to execute, provided unknown risk coverage, and had a high degree of redundancy.

To kick off the testing transformation initiative with easily-demonstrable test automation gains, they focused on automating a small set of critical test cases that were hand-selected by the business analysts. They implemented this test automation using Model-Based Test Automation because:

- It was the fastest way to get tests automated (it did not require assigning developers to testing or training testers to learn scripting)
- It relieved them of the "maintenance burden" that undermined their previous test automation attempts

Risk-Based Prioritization and Test Design

Next, they performed the risk assessment outlined in Chapter 3, and they found that these initial tests achieved approximately 40% business risk coverage. That's a great start—but remember that the product they are testing is a core banking solution. The stakes are extremely high, so they were committed to achieving much greater risk coverage. They used the test design methodology explained in Chapter 4 to rapidly increase the risk coverage with the minimal number of additional tests.

Many of these new tests were implemented at the API level because this approach allowed them to start testing earlier ("shift left") as well as execute tests much faster. As a rule of thumb, tests that validated the underlying business logic were implemented at the API level, and tests that validated specific parts of the interface were added at the UI level. With the first phase of this new approach, risk coverage increased to approximately 75%.

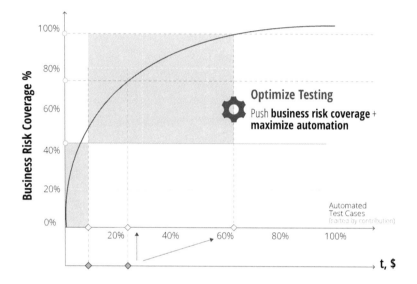

Over the next few months, they incrementally introduced additional test cases that pushed the risk coverage up to 95%.

Test Data Management

This powerful test suite created another challenge: in order to continuously execute the sophisticated new tests designed to increase their risk coverage, they needed very precise test data—and they needed valid data to be available at each test step, every time the tests executed. They tackled this challenge by synthetically generating the bulk of the test data that they needed, then supplementing it with some very specific production data that was masked in accordance with GDPR regulations.

Both synthetically-generated and masked production data is managed in a stateful way to ensure that no matter how many times a given test runs, it always has access to appropriate test data at every point in the testing process. This is accomplished using the strategies discussed in the previous chapter.

CI/CD Integration

With the test data challenge addressed, they could feasibly execute these automated tests during their CI process—so they integrated testing into their DevOps toolchain via Jenkins.

At this point, they had introduced risk-based prioritization and test design, increased test automation and expanded it from UI testing into API testing, implemented a core level of test data management, and set up testing to provide fast feedback on each build.

Service Virtualization

Over time, they noticed that test environment issues were causing a sizeable number of false positives and incomplete tests. Some tests interacted with dependent systems (e.g., third-party financial service APIs) that were unstable, or evolving in parallel with the part of the application that the team was responsible for testing. By applying service virtualization to simulate the behavior of these connected systems, they could consistently and reliably execute their end-to-end tests—no matter what state the actual dependent systems were in at any given time.

Exploratory Testing

Finally, they introduced exploratory testing as an additional "sanity check" that would help them expose risks that automated testing just wouldn't find. This includes usability issues, missing requirements, and risks lurking beyond the primary application paths that are the target of specification-based testing.

Note that this is *not* the exact path described in the model that I presented above—and that's completely fine. Some organizations might be so eager to achieve test automation that they may decide to make it the primary focus of their first phase of testing transformation. Others might start off by performing a risk assessment and applying test design to optimize the risk coverage of their manual tests. And many might begin by using exploratory testing to more rapidly expose critical issues in the functionality that's currently evolving the fastest. One size does not fit all. If your approach is tailored to your organization's specific needs, it will be easier to gain internal support, and your path to success should be much smoother.

It took approximately a year to achieve true adoption of all of these practices across the groups involved in the initial adoption. Rolling it out across the entire organization took another year and a half. Your own journey won't necessarily follow this exact path or these precise timelines. However, I wanted to provide some specifics to help you understand how all the elements of Continuous Testing might be rolled out in a real environment.

Results

Your results will vary, of course—but here's a quick look at what they have achieved so far:

- Test automation increased significantly with business domain experts creating and maintaining their own automated tests
- Regression, usability, business flow, interface, and migration testing is performed for each release
- Test assets are reused across technologies
- Extreme reuse enables rapid test creation and updating
- Tests are automatically parameterized with the optimal data combinations
- Developers receive quality feedback in minutes, not months
- Automated test results are trusted now that false positives are controlled

- 60% of defects are discovered in sprint
- 2X more defects are detected—with 44% fewer tests and no additional testing costs

Measuring Your Progress

The best way to expand an initiative is to demonstrate the quantifiable gains achieved at each step and set realistic targets for the next milestone. Appendix D presents some Continuous Testing KPIs you can use to quantify and demonstrate your progress in terms of accelerated innovation, reduced business risks, and improved cost efficiency.

CHAPTER 8

On the Death of Testing… and Wildebeests

Almost a decade ago, Albert Savoia walked on stage at the Google Test Automation Conference (GTAC) dressed as the Grim Reaper. With the Doors' *This is the End* playing in the background, Savoia famously declared testing dead. Dead were the days of developers delivering crappy code, then waiting for QA to test it and decide when it was finally fit for release. Instead, he suggested, we should deliver immediately and test in production. See what issues arise, then roll back the deployment if something severe occurs.

Are we there yet? Is the idea of testing a release before sending it out into the wild really dead? To answer that question, let's consider another example that involves death and the wild: the annual wildebeest migration in Africa.

Every year, over a million wildebeest migrate between Tanzania and Kenya. Along the way, they must cross the crocodile-infested Mara river. As you can imagine, this is a rather high-risk activity. As mentioned earlier, risk is the probability of a damaging event occurring, multiplied by the potential damage that could result from that event. In this case, the probability of facing one of the many huge crocodiles who are lurking in the river, anticipating the best feast of the entire year, is relatively high. The potential damage—death—is extremely high.

The riskiness of this situation would dramatically decrease if the crocodiles in the river were cute little 7-10 inch baby crocs instead of monstrous 17-23 foot adults. Even if the probability of encountering a crocodile remains the same, the potential damage diminishes tremendously. At worst, the baby crocs might nip at the wildebeests' feet or make their path across the river just a little bit bumpy.

What does this have to do with the death of software testing? Quite a lot, actually. If you want to rapidly release untested software into production, you need to be aware of what level of risk this involves, then consider whether that level of risk is acceptable to your business. As you can see from the large crocs versus the baby ones, all risks are not created equal.

If you're a social media platform updating the Recommended Friends algorithm, there's not much risk involved in moving fast and breaking things. Even if there's a high probability of users encountering issues, the impact to the business is extremely low. It's probably equal to, or even less than, little baby crocodiles nipping at the wildebeests' feet.

On the other hand, now imagine that you're responsible for the back-end systems that control business-critical operations such as financial transactions or energy delivery. You won't have nearly as many users as the social media platform, but any failure that does occur would be extremely critical and damaging.

Since the risk with the theoretical social media platform is low, they can get away with crossing the river without first "testing the waters," so to speak. If they're working on more critical functionality—for example, something that impacts their advertising revenue—they might want to be a little more cautious and creative. In that case, they might decide to perform an incremental user deployment. Essentially, this is like sending a small, low-priority group across the river first, then sending increasingly more (and more important) users over the river as long as no major "crocs" are surfacing.

With an application that the business depends on, you simply can't afford to send even a small group of users over untested waters. The risks—like the adult crocs—are huge and potentially devastating.

In summary, if you can truly afford to send users across untested waters, then maybe you can declare testing dead. However, if you're working on essential enterprise software and you try to survive by "testing in production" alone, it's *your business* that might end up dead—killed by those crocs.

APPENDIX A

Appendix A:
Who Should Be Testing?

What's the difference between a developer, a tester, and an SDET (software development engineer in test)?

This isn't a lead-in to a joke. In fact, it's a very serious question that's being debated across the software development community. Agile and DevOps adoption has blurred the historical distinction between testers and developers…and that's a good thing. When all goes well, developers are testing more and taking a greater responsibility for quality. Testers start designing tests early in each sprint and are constantly "in the loop" thanks to co-location and daily standups. If all goes well, fewer defects are introduced into the code base, and the role of "tester" is elevated from finding the manifestations of developers' mistakes to protecting the end-user experience.

However, there's a great debate stirring about how much testing responsibility should be transferred to developers—and how important it is for testers to know programming. I think that both of these proposed "mergers" (developers becoming testers and testers becoming programmers) threaten to undermine the goals of Agile and DevOps. Here's why:

1. Beyond GAFAs, asking developers to be testers impacts innovation velocity

If you're Google, Apple, Facebook, or Amazon (GAFA), you'll always have a constant supply of top talent ready to help you get innovations to the market at lightning speed. If you need to accelerate existing projects or launch new ones, you can pick and choose among the world's top developers. You can even get away with placing top-tier developers in an SDET role. Many eager developers will bear this not-so-ideal position in hopes of one day becoming a full-fledged developer at their dream employer.

However, in large enterprises, you usually don't have the luxury of top-tier developers knocking on your door. Attracting and retaining valuable developers is an ongoing struggle. As a result, it's hard enough to satisfy the business's insatiable demand for software when all your potential developers are focused on developing. You simply can't afford to have developers focused on the high-level testing tasks that professional testers can handle just as well…if not better.

2. The leanest test automation approaches don't require programming skills

Development methods have already become much leaner and more lightweight to help teams meet expectations for more software, faster. Testing technologies have also advanced—with lightweight scriptless approaches architected for the rapid change endemic in Agile and DevOps. However, many teams are still clinging to the mindset that test automation requires the high-maintenance, script-based testing approach that was introduced decades ago—but is still delivering underwhelming results (20% automation rates, at best). Across virtually all industries, people embrace software that enables advanced degrees of automation by abstracting the level of complexity. It's time for the software testing industry to accept this as well.

In Tricentis' research at enterprise environments across various industries, we've found that scriptless approaches yield significantly greater degrees of sustainable automation than scripted approaches. Moreover, they also remove the most common testing bottlenecks that trouble teams because:

1. They broaden the range of team members who can contribute to testing,
2. They're easier to keep in sync with evolving applications due to high reusability and modularity, and
3. They relieve you from having to maintain a "test" code base designed solely to test your actual code base.

3. You'll fail faster with both developers and testers testing

I guarantee that if you have both developers and professional testers testing, you will expose critical issues faster—and we're all familiar with the curve that shows how the time, cost, and effort of resolving defects rises exponentially over time. Detecting each defect as soon as it's feasible to do so has a tremendous impact on in-sprint velocity, as well as preventing field-reported defects from derailing future sprints.

"Development testing" is ideal for exposing coding errors. It involves checking the functionality and stability of the code that's written to implement a user story. This is critical. If some low-level mistake entered the code base (for a simplistic example, a multiplier with a misplaced decimal point), it's much more efficient to find and diagnose that problem with a direct unit test than an end-to-end test that checks functionality from the user perspective.

However, if your testing is primarily comprised of "bottom-up" tests designed by engineers, you're likely to overlook critical issues that your end users probably will *not* overlook. Does the new functionality work seamlessly within broader end-to-end transactions? If the user exercises the application in ways that the developers didn't anticipate, will the application respond in a reasonable manner? Does your functionality properly interact with the full range of behavior that dependencies might exhibit? With professional testers rigorously exercising core functionality in the context of a realistic business transaction (and from the "top-down" perspective of the end user), you will inevitably discover a host of issues that would otherwise go unnoticed until production.

When developers test in concert with professional testers, you'll get a much sharper understanding of the business risks associated with the release. You'll also gain the opportunity to resolve high-risk issues before your users ever encounter them. This is the ultimate goal of testing—and it requires more collaboration among roles, not more developer<>tester controversy.

Appendix B: Your Eroding Test Pyramid

It's hard to dispute that the test pyramid is the ideal model for Agile teams. Unit tests form a solid foundation for understanding whether new code is working correctly:

- **They achieve high code coverage:** The developer who wrote the code is uniquely qualified to cover that code as efficiently as possible. It's easy for the responsible developer to understand what's not yet covered and create test methods that fill the gaps.
- **They are fast and "cheap":** Unit tests can be written quickly, execute in seconds, and require only simple test harnesses (versus the more extensive test environments needed for system tests).
- **They are deterministic:** When a unit test fails, it's relatively easy to identify what code must be reviewed and fixed. It's like looking for a needle in a handful of hay versus trying to find a needle in a heaping haystack.

However, there's a problem with this model: the bottom falls out when you shift from *progression* to *regression* testing. Your test pyramid becomes a diamond.

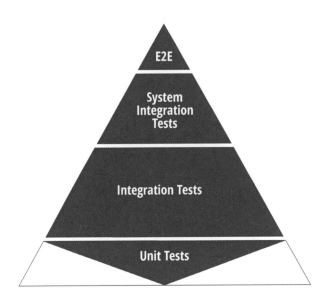

At least, that's what surfaced in the data we recently collected when monitoring unit testing practices across mature Agile teams. In each sprint, developers are religious about writing the tests required to validate each user story. Typically, it's unavoidable: passing unit tests are a key part of the "definition of done." By the end of most sprints, there's a solid base of new unit tests that are critical in determining if the new code is implemented correctly and meets expectations. These tests can cover approximately 70% of the new code.

From the next sprint on, these tests become regression tests. Little by little, they start failing—eroding the number of *working* unit tests at the base of the test pyramid, and eroding the level of risk coverage that the test suite once provided. After a few iterations, the same unit tests that once achieved 70% risk coverage provide only 50% coverage of that original functionality. This drops to 35% after several more iterations, and it typically degrades to 25% by the time 6 months have elapsed.

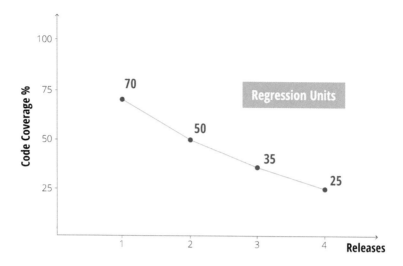

This subtle erosion can be extremely dangerous if you're fearlessly changing code, expecting those unit tests to serve as your safety net.

Why Unit Tests Erode

Unit tests erode for a number of reasons. Even though unit tests are theoretically more stable than other types of tests (e.g., UI tests), they too will inevitably start failing over time. Code gets extended, refactored, and repaired as the application evolves. In many cases, the implementation changes are significant enough to warrant unit test updates. Other times, the code changes expose the fact that the original test methods and test harness were too tightly coupled to the technical implementation—again, requiring unit test updates.

However, those updates aren't always made. After developers check in the tests for a new user story, they're under pressure to pick up and complete another user story. And another. And another. Each of those new user stories need passing unit tests to be considered done—but what happens if the "old" user stories start failing? Usually, nothing. The developer who wrote that code will have moved on, so he or she would need to get reacquainted with the long-forgotten code, diagnose why the test is failing, and figure out how to fix it. This isn't trivial, and it can disrupt progress on the current sprint.

Frankly, unit test maintenance often presents a burden that many developers truly resent. Just scan Stack Overflow and similar communities for countless developer frustrations related to unit test maintenance.

How to Stabilize the Erosion

I know that some exceptional organizations require—and allocate appropriate resources for—unit test upkeep. However, these tend to be organizations with the luxury of SDETs and other development resources dedicated to testing. Many enterprises are already struggling to deliver the volume and scope of software that the business expects, and they simply can't afford to shift development resources to additional testing.

If your organization lacks the development resources required for continuous unit test maintenance, what can you do? One option is to have testers compensate for the lost risk coverage through resilient tests that they can create and control. Professional testers recognize that designing and maintaining tests is their primary job, and that they are ultimately evaluated by the success and effectiveness of the test suite. Let's be honest. Who's more likely to keep tests current: the developers who are pressured to deliver more code faster, or the testers who are rewarded for finding major issues (or blamed for overlooking them)? In the most successful organizations we studied, testers offset the risk coverage loss from eroding unit tests by adding integration-level tests—primarily at the API level, when feasible. This enables them to restore the degrading "change-detection safety net" without disrupting developers' progress on the current sprint.

APPENDIX C

Appendix C: What About Our TCoE?

Just a few years ago, global enterprises started clamoring to get Testing Centers of Excellence (TCoEs) in place. In 2011, only 4% of organizations had TCoEs…but 80% wanted TCoEs. By 2015, nearly half of Global 2000 organizations adopted TCoEs—a staggering 825% rise in just 4 years. These TCoEs promised to increase efficiency by establishing a command center that was laser focused on standardizing software testing methodology, best practices, automation, KPIs, metrics, and toolsets across the organization.

Then along came Agile.

Even though Agile adoption has been steadily rising for over a decade, it is just now reaching the majority of development projects in large enterprises. It is taking even longer to impact how these projects are tested. Usually, the focus is on development—until it becomes clear that you can't meet your acceleration goals without transforming testing as well as development. As legacy testing approaches are (eventually) reassessed, the value and future of TCoEs are also brought into question:

Are TCoEs holding us back, or can they help us move forward?

I believe that TCoEs can help transform your testing process—but only if they first undergo their own digital transformation.

The Structure of Traditional TCoEs

Before we start dissecting which parts of a traditional TCoE help and hurt Agile testing goals, let's first focus on what a typical TCoE looks like. At the top, there's a TCoE head, then a number of test architects and managers reporting to him or her.

Three additional roles then report directly to the test architects and managers:

- **Test design specialists:** People in this role help the organization plan and define the optimal set of test cases. Although this is a proven way to increase test efficiency, very few organizations currently have specialists in this role.

- **Manual testers:** These people manually execute the defined test scenarios and document the results at each step. This is, by far, the most common role in the TCoE. It is usually outsourced to Global System Integrators.

- **Automation engineers:** In organizations that have achieved some level of test automation, these individuals are the ones responsible for defining and maintaining that test automation.

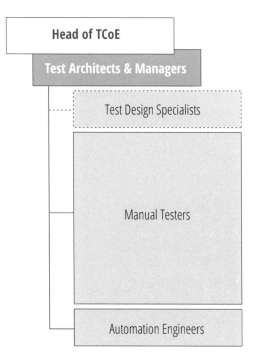

How Traditional TCoEs Impede Agile

When organizations attempt to use a traditional TCoE to meet the new business expectations associated with Agile, a number of issues tend to arise:

- **Latency delays testing:** Testing does not begin until a project is completed and "thrown over the wall" to the QA team for testing. This means that developers don't receive feedback until weeks or months after they've completed a development task. This latency complicates defect resolution, increases rework, and delays time to market.

- **Testing is too slow:** With Agile, the application is built (at least) daily and new functionality is ready to be tested every few days. Manual test execution simply cannot keep pace with the rapid rate of change.

Month-long test cycles are no longer feasible once developers transition to Agile sprints, which are two weeks or shorter.

- **Testing and development are miles away:** Agile expects testers to collaborate closely with developers in order to provide the rapid feedback needed to "fail fast." Without co-location in a cross-functional team, testers have limited insight into the business and technical issues associated with each user story. Moreover, distances mean delays in asking/answering questions, reproducing defects, and so forth.

TCoE Aspects That Could Help Enterprise Agile Testing

Despite these issues, we don't need to throw out the baby with the bathwater. Two primary TCoE benefits—standardization and governance—can be quite beneficial when introducing and scaling Agile across a large Global 2000 organization:

- **Standardization:** Standardization of methodology and techniques is a proven way to increase efficiency. Standardizing on core test design, test data design, and test automation practices—while still providing each team a reasonable level of freedom— significantly reduces overhead and "waste." The resulting efficiency gain helps testers deliver the fast feedback expected with Agile.

- **Governance:** To continuously optimize Agile processes, it's important to aggregate KPI and other metrics into a comprehensive top-level report that crosses business units. This is only possible if the various teams ensure that their unique metrics are compatible with higher-level reporting expectations.

Digital TCoEs: A New Path Forward

I've found that a new approach to a TCoE—what I call a Digital TCoE—enables enterprise organizations to satisfy the changing business demands associated with Agile initiatives... without losing their grip on the standardization and governance critical for process optimization and scalability.

The structure of the Digital TCoE is fundamentally different than that of a traditional TCoE. Like before, we start with the Head of the Digital TCoE at the top, followed by a layer of test architects and managers, then some test design specialists and automation engineers that help the testers maximize the efficiency and effectiveness of their testing.

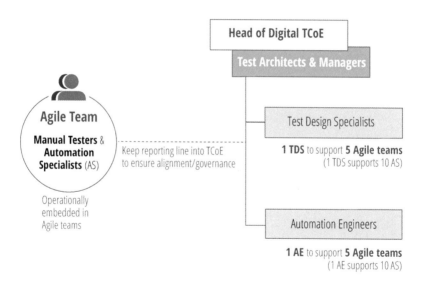

However, there is one major structural difference: we no longer have manual testers sitting in the TCoE. Instead, testers are operationally embedded within cross-functional Agile teams (ideally, 2 testers in a team with 5-6 developers), but still reporting up to test architects and managers in the

TCoE to ensure appropriate alignment and governance. The testers are fully supported by the TCoE in terms of tooling, training, technical customizations, and so on.

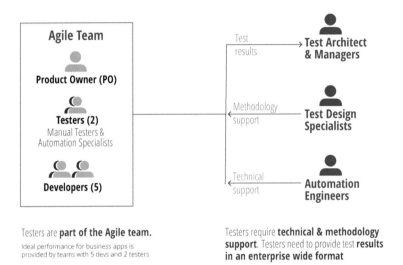

Testers are **part of the Agile team.**
Ideal performance for business apps is provided by teams with 5 devs and 2 testers

Testers require **technical & methodology support**. Testers need to provide test **results in an enterprise wide format**

This co-location is obviously a big change for testers—but it pales in comparison to the changes in the type of testing they are performing. To meet business expectations for accelerated delivery and continuous quality feedback, test automation suddenly rises from "nice-to-have" to "must-have." Simply situating testers next to developers is not sufficient; test*ing*, as well as test*ers*, must be an integral part of the Agile team. This means that testing must become an organic part of getting each user story to "done done" rather than a late-stage activity tacked on every month or so.

In response, enabling rapid, efficient test automation becomes a primary goal of the core Digital TCoE structure. Automation engineers become critical for guiding testers on how to automate testing, and test design specialists help them assess what specific test cases are most important to create and automate. Scriptless test automation tools reduce the learning curve

What about Federated TCoEs and Communities of Practice?

This concept of Digital TCoEs is similar to what Forrester calls a *Federated TCoE* and Gartner calls a *Community of Practice*. In *The State of Agile*, Forrester VP and Principal Analyst Diego lo Giudice recommends: "Start by assigning full-time testers with full-stack development skills to your cross-functional teams: 69% of expert firms do this, compared with 57% of neophytes. Then, help dev teams grow their automation levels and scope with a few centrally-managed automation engineers: 34% of expert firms do this, versus 20% of neophytes. Federate competencies from the TCoE by keeping highly specialized functional, performance, security, service virtualization, and test data management (TDM) experts as centralized resources for intellectual property (IP) creation and consulting."

The Digital TCoE, Federated TCoE, and Community of Practice concepts all focus on fostering learning and knowledge sharing among their members. The main difference with Gartner's Community of Practice is that it places less emphasis on governance and reporting. It is less structured—and more fluid. Gartner's IT Glossary defines a Community of Practice as "people associated and interlinked in a communication or knowledge network because of their shared interest or shared responsibility for a subject area. Examples are people who hold similar job functions (project managers, department managers, team leaders or customer service agents); all the people on a project team; and people interested in specific technologies (e-commerce or network management). Communities continually emerge and dissolve, and their membership, processes and knowledge continually change and evolve."

and help testers, who are typically business domain experts (not programmers), make their testing efforts faster and repeatable. This enables the team to achieve the expected level of test automation without losing the domain expertise that's critical for exposing critical defects—and ensuring that rapid, iterative releases do not ultimately compromise the end user experience.

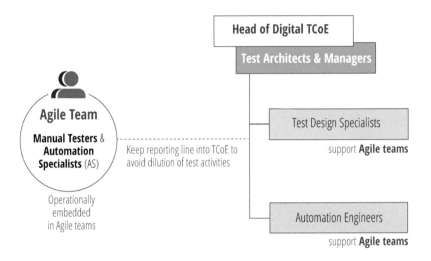

The Digital TCoE <> tester relationship involves both give and take. On the one hand, the Digital TCoE supports the testers in the Agile teams from both a methodology and an automation standpoint. On the other hand, testers are expected to provide the TCoE reports in a standardized way so that they can be aggregated for enterprise-wide reporting—enabling governance for test results.

APPENDIX D

Appendix D:
KPIs for Measuring Your Progress

As I mentioned in Chapter 7, the best way to expand an initiative is to demonstrate the quantifiable gains achieved at each step and set realistic targets for the next milestone. Here are some Continuous Testing KPIs you can use to quantify and demonstrate your progress in terms of accelerated innovation, reduced business risks, and improved cost efficiency.

QUALITY

8 Risk coverage %

$$\sum_{req} f(frequency, damage)$$

9 Requirements coverage %

$$(\frac{\# Requirements}{Total Requirements}) \times 100$$

10 Code coverage %

$$(\frac{Lines\ of\ code\ executed}{Total\ lines\ of\ code}) \times 100$$

11 Mean time to detect (MTTD)

$$\frac{Defects\ found}{Total\ execution\ time}$$

12 Defect leakage %

$$(\frac{Defects\ slipped}{Total\ defects}) \times 100$$

13 Defect rejection %

$$(\frac{Defects\ rejected}{Total\ defects\ found}) \times 100$$

14 Tests passed %

$$(\frac{Test\ cases\ passed}{Total\ test\ cases}) \times 100$$

15 Product downtime %

$$\frac{Product\ downtime}{Total\ run\ time}$$

16 Defects found by automation/ manual ratio

$$\frac{Defects\ found\ by\ automation}{Defects\ found\ by\ manual\ testing}$$

17 Average defects per exploratory session

$$\frac{Defects\ found}{\#\ of\ sessions}$$

18 Defect distribution by

- Priority
- Severity
- Functional area
- Test type/stage (dev, QA, UAT, End User)
- Cause (env, architecture, code, design, requirements, user entry)
- Test type (review, walkthrough, test execution, exploratory, etc.)

COST

19 Cost of defect by

- Severity
- Stage found (e.g. dev, QA, UAT, production)

20 Cost of test environment

- Hardware
- Software

21 Cost of environment maintenance

- Hardware
- Software

22 Cost of test creation

- Manual
- Automated

23 Cost of test maintenance

- Manual
- Automated

24 Cost of test execution

- Manual
- Automated

25 Average cost per tester

$$\frac{Total\ tester\ cost}{\#\ of\ testers}$$

References and Related Resources

Direct links to the references cited in this book, as well as related resources such as real-world Continuous Testing success stories, are available at https://www.tricentis.com/CTbook.

Wolfgang Platz is the Founder and Chief Product Officer of Tricentis. Wolfgang is the force behind innovations such as model-based automation and the linear expansion test design methodology. The technology he developed drives Tricentis' Continuous Testing Platform, which is recognized as the industry's #1 solution by all top analysts. Today, he is responsible for advancing Tricentis' vision to make resilient enterprise automation a reality across Global 2000 organizations.

Prior to Tricentis, Wolfgang was at Capgemini as a group head of IT development for one of the world's largest IT insurance-development projects. There, he was responsible for architecture and implementation of life insurance policies and project management for several projects in banks.

Wolfgang holds a Master's degree in Technical Physics as well as a Master's degree in Business Administration from the Vienna University of Technology.

Made in the USA
Lexington, KY
09 December 2019